CAROL VORDERMAN
English Made Easy

10
Minutes
A Day
Vocabulary

Ages
7–11

DK

Author Linda Ruggieri
Consultant Claire White

10-minute challenge

Try to complete the exercises for each topic in 10 minutes or less. Note the time it takes you in the "Time taken" column below.

Penguin Random House

DK London
Editors Elizabeth Blakemore, Jolyon Goddard
Senior Editor Deborah Lock
Managing Editor Christine Stroyan
Managing Art Editor Anna Hall
Consultant Claire White
Senior Production Editor Andy Hilliard
Senior Production Controller Jude Crozier
Jacket Design Development Manager Sophia MTT
Publisher Andrew Macintyre
Associate Publishing Director Liz Wheeler
Art Director Karen Self
Publishing Director Jonathan Metcalf

DK Delhi
Senior Editor Rupa Rao
Editor Rohini Deb
Art Editors Tanvi Nathyal, Yamini Panwar
Managing Editors Soma B. Chowdhury, Kingshuk Ghoshal
Managing Art Editors Ahlawat Gunjan, Govind Mittal
DTP Designers Anita Yadav, Rakesh Kumar, Harish Aggarwal
Senior Jacket Designer Suhita Dharamjit
Jackets Editorial Coordinator Priyanka Sharma

This edition published in 2020
First published in Great Britain in 2015 by
Dorling Kindersley Limited
One Embassy Gardens, 8 Viaduct Gardens,
London, SW11 7BW

Copyright © 2015, 2020 Dorling Kindersley Limited
A Penguin Random House Company
10 9
011-270528-Apr/2020

A CIP catalogue record for this book
is available from the British Library.
ISBN: 978-0-2411-8385-4

Printed and bound in Scotland

All images © Dorling Kindersley.
For further information see: www.dkimages.com

For the curious
www.dk.com

Contents

Time taken

Time filler:
In these boxes are some extra challenges to extend your skills. You can do them if you have some time left after finishing the questions. Or, these can be stand-alone activities that you can do in 10 minutes.

Words and their definitions

Figuring out the meaning of words as you read will ensure you have a better understanding of text.

1 Draw lines to match the words in the top row with the words that mean the same or almost the same in the bottom row.

exciting   power   choose   exchange

strength   swap   thrilling   select

2 What does the underlined word in each sentence mean? Pick your answer from the box below.

| purchased | correct | grew well | a great number |

The farm produced an abundance of apples this year. ....

The apple trees thrived because of the rain. ....

We bought two baskets of apples. ....

Your description of the problem is accurate. ....

3 Use words from the box to complete the sentences below.

| cupcake | lemon | sandpaper | snake | joke |

Something that tastes sour is a ....

Something that feels rough is ....

Something that is scrumptious is a ....

Something that slithers is a ....

Something that is amusing is a ....

Time filler:
Create a personal flip-book dictionary listing words and their definitions. You could also add pictures. It will be a quick and easy reference for tricky words you want to remember.

④ Read the first word in each row below. Then circle the two words in that row that mean the same as the first word.

end	finish	part	conclude
show	destroy	display	demonstrate

⑤ Read the clues below to complete the crossword puzzle.
Hint: the first letter for each word in the crossword has been provided.

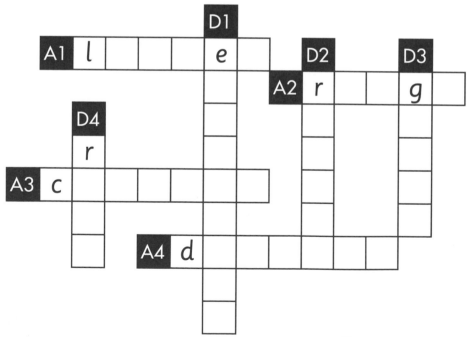

Across

1. To delay going somewhere

2. Having an irregular or uneven surface

3. Being able to do something

4. To wreck or ruin

Down

1. Very good

2. To mend something

3. To move smoothly and silently

4. Unusual

Antonyms

An antonym is a word that has an opposite meaning to another word. For example, "early" is the opposite of "late".

1 Use words from the box to write an antonym for each word listed below.

> down   day   full   evening   dry   sad   fake   fiction
>
> smooth   soft   bad   below   dark   serious   close

open   ....

good   ....

up   ....

real   ....

light   ....

hard   ....

funny   ....

night   ....

rough   ....

happy   ....

morning   ....

fact   ....

above   ....

empty   ....

wet   ....

2 Write the letter **A** in the box if the pairs of words are antonyms.

near/far   ☐

lengthy/long   ☐

ask/answer   ☐

hate/love   ☐

little/small   ☐

narrow/thin   ☐

large/small   ☐

baby/adult   ☐

Time filler:
Write a poem to describe a person, place, pet, thing or experience, using antonyms in each line. For example, the first line could be: My dog makes me **happy** when I am **sad**.

(3) Write an antonym for the underlined word in each sentence.

This watch was so <u>cheap</u>.   ....

His drawing was colourful and <u>bright</u>.   ....

We drove down a <u>straight</u> country road.   ....

Did you have a good <u>morning</u>?   ....

Our group agreed to be <u>united</u>.   ....

The purple stone in my ring is a <u>common</u> one.   ....

(4) Find an antonym for each of the clues below to solve the crossword puzzle. **Hint:** the first letter for each antonym has been given in the crossword.

Across

1. old   ....

2. lowest   ....

3. take   ....

4. go   ....

Down

1. rude   ....

2. wild   ....

Adjectives

An adjective is a describing word. Adjectives are added to nouns to give more detail or information and can make writing more interesting.

1 Read the story below. Then underline the 14 adjectives in it.

Baby's busy day

The prince and princess travelled to faraway places, where they met large crowds of friendly people. People always asked about their adorable baby. They would ask, "Where is beautiful Andrew?"

One day, the prince and princess took Andrew to visit babies. He wore a blue shirt and white trousers. He was happy to see all the little babies. He enjoyed playing with the different toys, too.

Then the prince and princess took Andrew home. He had had a busy day. He fell into a deep sleep. He dreamed about his lovely day and all his new friends.

Which adjectives in the story tell you about the size of something?

....

Which adjectives in the story describe Andrew?

....

2 Choose the most suitable adjective from the box for each sentence.

clumsy	noisy	sporty	lazy

The .... lawn mower woke me up.

My .... dog likes to sleep all day.

Your new car is so ...., unlike your old piece of junk!

She was so .... that she bumped into the table.

Time filler:
Sketch a picture of yourself on a large piece of drawing paper. Write the word "Me" at the top. Then write adjectives that describe yourself on the picture.

(3) Underline the adjective in each sentence below. Then write a word that means the same as that adjective. You can use a dictionary for help.

The mischievous puppy fell asleep on the sofa. ....

We could not work out the cryptic message he sent. ....

The miniature doll's house had many rooms. ....

The clever children knew how to find help. ....

(4) Read the words in each box. Then underline the adjective.

delicious damage delete	illness illustrated isolate	elegant effort electricity	brilliant breathe branch
agitate ancient amuse	mystery moist mingle	flake filthy fever	squatter species sensible

Choose an adjective from above to match each definition below.

old ....   has pictures ....

dazzling ....   graceful ....

tasty ....   reasonable ....

slightly wet ....   very dirty ....

Adverbs

An adverb is a word that modifies the meaning of a verb. It tells you **where**, **when** or **how** an action is performed. Many adverbs end in **ly**.

(1) Underline the adverb in each sentence. Then write "where", "how" or "when" to show the use of the adverb in that sentence.

My friend writes to me often. ....

Keila boastfully described her family holiday. ....

Did you travel far to get to the meeting? ....

Jack will come to the game tomorrow. ....

The little boy ate his ice cream noisily. ....

The dog barked so the birds flew away. ....

(2) Underline the adverb in each sentence. Then circle the word it modifies.

You can easily make a sandwich for lunch.

I like cereal but my sister mostly eats toast in the morning.

I totally believe what you say.

Let's discuss this privately in my room.

(3) Draw lines to match each adjective to its adverb and then each adverb to its meaning.

Adjective	Adverb	Definition
day	daily	not clearly
obscure	privately	every day
private	obscurely	in a secret way

Time filler:
Create a word search with adverbs from these two pages. Write synonyms or other clues for the adverbs, such as "regularly" or "frequently" for the word "often" and "all the time" for the word "always".

(4) Read each sentence and underline the adverb in it.
Then write each adverb under its description below.

Kevin nervously waited for his turn to spell the next word.

Jane had never been to an amusement park.

Franco cheerfully whistled as he walked home.

Gina played the piano well during her recital.

Paolo quickly ran across the road to get help from a policeman.

Dave carelessly ran on the wet floor and slipped.

rapidly	without care	not ever
....	....	....
anxiously	happily	with skill
....	....	....

(5) Change the words in the box to adverbs and use them to complete the sentences.

loud	elegant	obvious	main

The lady .... walked across the red carpet.

I didn't realise that I was speaking ....

The land was .... used for farming.

The team was .... nervous about playing.

Contractions

A contraction is formed by combining two words into one and replacing one or more letters with an apostrophe. For example, "we are" becomes "we're" and "I have" becomes "I've".

① Write the contraction for each pair of words.

she is _____	you are _____	does not _____	I am _____
he is _____	we are _____	do not _____	he would _____
it is _____	they are _____	there is _____	let us _____

② Both "had" and "have" can be combined with different words to make contractions. Write the contraction for each combination.

had

we had ....

he had ....

you had ....

I had ....

have

you have ....

they have ....

we have ....

I have ....

③ Rewrite these sentences by changing each contraction into its long form.

I don't believe you.

....

You aren't concentrating on your work.

....

She hasn't called yet.

....

We aren't going to the party.

....

Time filler:
Play a game to see if you and a friend or
a family member can hold a conversation
for 10 minutes without using any contractions.
The first one to use one loses!

(4) Two friends are talking. How does their speech sound?
Write the contraction for the underlined words in each sentence.

Maya: What is going on, Kate? ....

Kate: My Dad is taking me to the new football pitch. ....

Maya: That is a good idea. ....

Kate: He is going to practise with me. It will be fun.
Would you like to join us? ....

Maya: I would love to! But I will have to ask my
parents first. ....

Kate: Great! Let us talk later. ....

(5) Contractions and possessives can be tricky to tell apart. "It's" is
a contraction of "it is", whereas "its" shows possession, or ownership.
Circle the correct word to complete each sentence below.

Whose / Who's going to the game?

Bob's / Bobs going to the game with me.

Its / It's the ticket for the game.

That's / Thats the team's logo.

There's / Theres no way to get there by train.

Comparisons

We use analogies, metaphors and similes to make comparisons. See if you can work through these questions as quick as a flash!

(1) Analogies often appear this way: drop : rain :: flake : snow.
They are read this way: drop is to rain as flake is to snow.
Write the word from the box that correctly completes each analogy.

room	food	shoes	car

horse : carriage :: motor : ....

hands : mittens :: feet : ....

shovel : dirt :: fork : ....

sky : Earth :: ceiling : ....

(2) Complete each analogy with the correct word from the box.

sad	sun	evening	down

Open is to close as up is to ....

Funny is to serious as happy is to ....

Dark is to light as shade is to ....

Dawn is to morning as dusk is to ....

(3) A metaphor is a comparison that does not use the word "like" or "as".
Circle the words that tell what is being described in each metaphor.

The road was a blanket of snow.

My teacher is a walking encyclopedia.

Last night, the motorway was a car park.

Time filler:
Write your own analogies and use them to quiz family members and friends. Try making them complicated or silly. For example: movie is to watch as book is to read.

④ A simile is a comparison that uses a word such as "like" or "as" to make the comparison. Find the words in the word search that complete the similes in the sentences below.

a	d	s	u	n	o	p	g	h	c	c	x	q
m	p	a	r	r	o	t	n	z	h	p	i	b
o	w	t	r	e	a	s	u	r	e	e	y	a
p	i	b	n	m	g	w	p	r	e	n	e	n
b	j	n	l	a	f	z	y	v	t	g	w	q
e	l	e	p	h	a	n	t	s	a	u	i	u
e	o	d	f	q	p	m	a	c	h	i	n	e
k	n	w	v	s	o	r	g	e	o	n	k	t

Her yellow dress is as bright as the ....

She squawked like a ....

The museum collection is like hidden ....

They walked like a herd of ....

The team worked like a well-oiled ....

He was as busy as a ....

He ran as fast as a ....

The little boy is walking like a ....

That lunch was like a ....

Homographs

Homographs are words that have the same spelling but different meanings. Sometimes, homographs have different pronunciations, too.

① Find and circle each pair of homographs in these pairs of sentences. Then underline the word that matches the definition on the right.

The record shows your licence has expired.

Did you record your brother's song?

| to reproduce sound |

The baby ran after the ball.

He wore a tuxedo to the ball.

| large, formal party |

② Pick the correct homograph from the box to complete each pair of sentences below.

| tear | bow | date | present |

Tie a .... in your hair.

Be sure to .... after you perform.

More than 20 people were .... at the meeting.

I want to open my birthday .... now!

That is the .... of my next dental appointment.

My brother is going on a .... with Becky tonight.

Why did you .... the pages out of the magazine?

We could see the .... on the actor's cheek.

Time filler:
Think of five pairs of homographs
and write silly sentences using the
words in each pair. For example:
the diamond mine is mine.

3) Draw a line to match the descriptions to the words they define.
Each word on the right has two meanings.

a winged mammal and a piece of sporting equipment   light

a drink to celebrate and browned slices of bread   date

sweet dark fruit and a day and time   hide

animal skin and to conceal   bat

not heavy and not dark   toast

4) Use each word from the box twice to complete the story.

| fine | park | bark | left | right | lead |

Trip to the park

Today, Dad drove us to the _____. We _____
home after lunch. The weather was _____. Ben, our
dog, began to _____ as Dad looked for somewhere to
_____ the car. Dogs are allowed to run free in the park.
In other public places, they must be kept on a _____ or you
might get a _____. In the park, we let Ben _____
the way to his favourite spot: the big pond. We came to a fork in the
path by a big tree with reddish brown _____. I wasn't sure
whether to turn _____ or _____, but Ben knew
which was the _____ way. Soon, we were at the pond
and Ben had a good swim.

Concept words

Some words can be sorted into groups because they are related in meaning. For example: "cloud", "rain", "snow" and "hail" are related to the concept, or idea, of "weather".

① In each column, circle one of the last two words to complete the group of concept words.

uncle	meadow	taxi	nose
father	field	train	mouth
brother	valley	bus	eyes
niece	**forest**	**ferry**	**ears**
nephew	**river**	**car**	**toes**

② Cross out the word in each row that is not related to the others.

dog	horse	cow	shark
frog	butterfly	moth	bee
window	tree	roof	door

③ Fill in a word to complete each concept group.

Subjects in school

history
maths
science
....

Coverings for feet

shoes
boots
sandals
....

④ Give a title to each of the two concept groups.

....

ant
bee
butterfly
moth

hawk
crow
owl
puffin

Time filler:
Sketch a picture of your classroom or school.
On the same page, write as many words
as you can think of that are related to
your school. Aim for at least 25 words!

⑤ Sort these words into the four boxes below based on the concepts
they refer to. Then write a title for each box.

processor	mouse	chain	flower	wheels
farm	root	keyboard	spokes	monitor	handlebars
leaf	harvest	stem	crops	irrigation

....

....

....

....

....

⑥ Read the words in the boxes below. Write a title for each box.

....

circumference

diameter

radius

centre

mane

forelock

hoof

tail

Shades of meaning

The meanings of some words are close
and have subtle, or small, differences.
It is useful to know these differences so
you can use the words correctly.

① Choose the correct word from the box to complete each row.

lukewarm	massive	angry	intelligent

grumpy	cross	furious	....
competent	smart	brilliant	....
big	huge	immense	....
tepid	warm	hot	....

② Put the groups of words in the correct order from weakest to strongest.
Write them from left to right in each row of boxes.

cold, freezing, cool	furious, annoyed, angry	dirty, filthy, soiled

▢ → ▢ → ▢

▢ → ▢ → ▢

▢ → ▢ → ▢

③ For each pair, circle the word that has a stronger meaning.

astound	surprise		soar	fly
trip	fall		call	yell
boil	simmer		slam	close

Time filler:
You may sometimes write that you are happy. But you can probably list several words that mean the same as "happy". See if you can think of 10 of them.

4 Solve the crossword puzzle below. The answers are close in their meaning to the clues. **Hint:** the first letter for each answer has been provided.

Across

1. icy

2. tired

3. be anxious

4. excited

Down

1. injured

2. sad

3. dislike

4. eat

(crossword grid with entries A1 f, A2 e, A3 w, A4 t, D1 h, D2 m, D3 l, D4 d)

5 Pick words from the crossword above to complete the sentences below.

Our players were .... when they beat the Royals.

Terry was .... when the match was cancelled.

She had to .... her lunch before going to class.

I just .... having to clean my room.

Joan .... herself when she fell down the stairs.

Useful word list 1

Read each column of words. Think about each word's meaning and then write a synonym on the line next to it. The first five have been done for you. Answers may vary.

accurate	correct	dainty	....
actual	real	damage	....
adjust	alter	decrease	....
advice	help	depth	....
affect	influence	difficult	....
baffle	....	educate	....
baggage	....	effort	....
catalogue	....	emotion	....
caution	....	fatal	....
certain	....	generous	....
chief	....	glisten	....
circular	....	guide	....
clumsy	....	harsh	....
daily	....	illustrate	....

23

Time filler:
There may have been a few words on these two pages that you couldn't think of a synonym for or were unfamiliar to you. Look in a dictionary or a thesaurus to help you finish the activity.

increase ....

jagged ....

lagoon ....

marvel ....

narrator ....

nation ....

observe ....

occasion ....

odour ....

official ....

often ....

pardon ....

permit ....

phrase ....

possess ....

recent ....

region ....

regular ....

remember ....

scent ....

seize ....

strange ....

strength ....

tablet ....

value ....

vapour ....

weary ....

wreck ....

Homophones

Homophones are words that
sound the same but have
different spellings and meanings.

① Read the pairs of homophones in the box below. Then choose
the correct homophone and write it next to its clue.

> whole/hole   aloud/allowed   scent/sent
>
> piece/peace   week/weak   threw/through

odour .... posted .... opening ....

tossed .... entire .... feeble ....

out loud .... permitted .... via ....

calm .... part of .... seven days ....

② Read aloud the pairs of homophones in the box below. Then
pick the correct homophone to complete each sentence.
Hint: only six words are needed.

> grate/great   doe/dough   flour/flower   break/brake   days/daze

Did you .... the cheese?

The .... seemed to fly by during our holiday.

The lady placed a pink .... in a blue vase on every table.

Joanna cried out when she saw her favourite toy ....

We used ...., eggs and milk to make the ....

Time filler:
Homophones can be tricky. Try writing some sentences that include pairs of homophones to help you remember their meanings. For example: Kate said aloud that she was allowed to go to the party.

3 Read each homophone and the clue. Then complete the crossword puzzle. **Hint:** the first letter for each answer has been provided.

Across

1. knight, evening

2. rays, increase

3. loan, one

4. seem, edge

Down

1. no, understand

2. horse, sounding husky

3. blew, colour

4. knows, we use it to smell

5. dew, owed

4 Complete the two charts below by writing the correct homophone for each word.

Word	Homophone
would	
threw	
their	

Word	Homophone
peak	
pale	
you're	

Visual information

Pictures sometimes help us understand the meaning of words better. Annotated pictures are very useful. They have labels showing you the different parts.

1) Look at the parts of a bicycle below. Then circle the correct answers in the questions that follow.

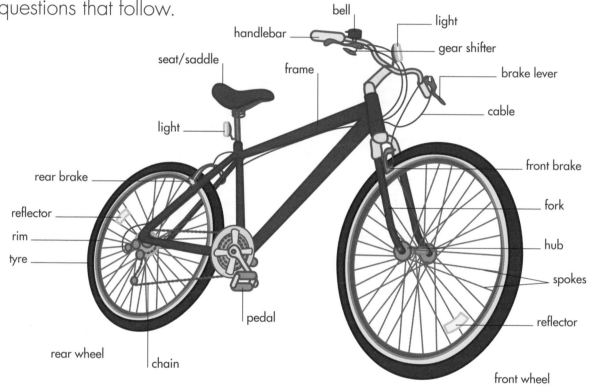

Which four parts of the bike are directly attached to the wheel?

spoke   rim   pedal   hub   tyre   saddle

Where is the bell?

on the handlebar

on the chain

What is the centre of the wheel called?

hub   rim

What is another name for the saddle?

tyre   seat

What is the largest part of the bicycle?

wheel   frame

(2) Look at the parts of a sailing boat below. Then circle the correct answers to the questions that follow.

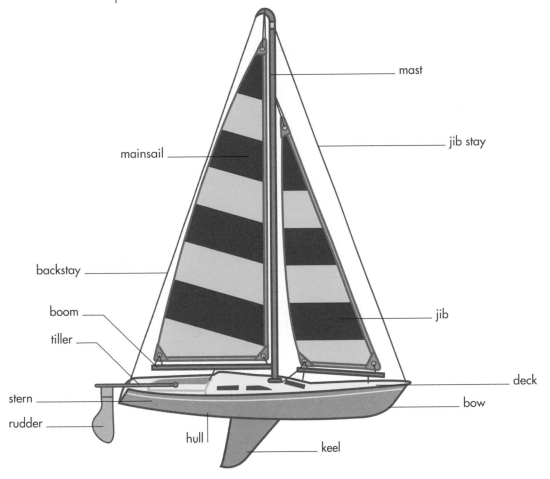

What is the front part of the boat called?   stern bow

Which part of the boat holds up the sail?   mast tiller

What is the larger sail on the boat called?   jib mainsail

Which underwater part keeps the boat stable?   jib keel

What is the main body of the boat known as?   hull boom

Science words

Some words are very specific to science. They are usually used only when writing or talking about science subjects, such as biology (the study of living things) or physics (the study of matter and energy).

1 Read the three words in each box. Then pick the phrase that best describes each group of words.

Kinds of habitat	Kinds of storm	Life cycle of a frog

egg tadpole adult	rainforest desert ocean	tornado hurricane blizzard

....

2 For each row of words, cross out the one word in it that is not related to the other words.

snake	tiger	turtle	crocodile
herbivore	prey	omnivore	carnivore
tide	currents	forest	ocean

3 Look at the groups of words in the table below. Label each group using the following key for each kind of science.
B – Biology **E** – Earth and space science
P – Physics **ET** – Engineering and technology

Words	Science	Words	Science
heart, brain, lungs		sound, light, heat	
computer, invention		rocks, oceans, stars	
force, friction		reptiles, mammals, fish	

Time filler:
Science words are interesting but can be quite challenging. Create a science glossary. List science words, especially those that are new to you. Draw pictures for each of them to help you remember them.

(4) Draw a line from the definition to the word it defines.

see-through	fish
gaseous state of water	transparent
two kinds of energy	vapour
large mass of ice	constellation
a group of stars	light and heat
animal with fins, scales and gills	omnivore
animal that eats plants and animals	glacier

(5) Choose the correct answer for each question from the box below.

> backbone   earthquake   camouflage
> thicker fur   collect data

What do some animals need to adapt to a cold environment?

....

What do some animals use to blend into their surroundings?

....

What might you do after conducting an experiment?

....

What does a vertebrate have?

....

What is an example of a natural disaster?

....

Word games

Word games are a fun way
to test your vocabulary skills.
Have a go at these magic
square games and then
check your answers.

In each magic square game, read the clues in the first word grid.
For each word, find its synonym or definition in the second word grid.
Then write the number of that word next to the letter that matches it in
the bottom grid. For example, the answer to the first clue, **A. precious**,
is **2. valuable**, so **A2** is the first full answer in the bottom grid. Check
your answers by making sure the numbers in the boxes add up to the
same number horizontally, vertically and diagonally. Magical, isn't it?

1 Magic square game 1

A. precious	B. confuse	C. uneven
D. model of the world	E. circular	F. bloom
G. attentive	H. delicate	I. go down

1. blossom	2. valuable	3. fragile
4. focused	5. round	6. jagged
7. perplex	8. descend	9. globe

A	B	C ....
D	E	F ....
G	H	I ....

Time filler:
Create your own word games.
Play them at home with your friends
or family to see who has the most
impressive vocabulary.

2 Magic square game 2

A. try	B. maintain	C. sturdy
D. conclude	E. delay	F. enclose
G. display	H. hysterical	I. foe

1. preserve	2. enemy	3. end
4. exhibit	5. postpone	6. strong
7. surround	8. attempt	9. frantic

A	B	C ....
D	E	F ....
G	H	I ....

Word meanings

In writing, an unusual word is often
explained, or defined, when it is first
used. At other times, the text may give
you clues to the word's meaning.

(1) In each pair of sentences below, circle the word in **bold** and
underline its meaning.

Our science teacher told us to wear long trousers to prevent bites from
insects and **ticks**. A tick is a tiny animal related to spiders.

Whales have **blubber** under their skin to keep them warm.
Blubber is a thick layer of fat.

Some animals protect themselves through **mimicry**. Using mimicry
means copying the appearance, actions or sounds of another animal.

(2) In each sentence below, circle the word in **bold** and underline
its meaning.

The storm caused a huge **surge**, or wave of water, to flood the town.

The picture was **askew**, or not straight, on the wall.

We hiked to the **summit**, the highest point, of the trail.

(3) Underline the examples given to help you understand the subject
of each sentence below.

Some rodents, including hamsters and gerbils, can be kept as pets.

Renewable energy, such as wind or solar power, comes from
natural resources.

Some biomes, including rainforests and deserts, are home to
unusual animals.

4 Read the sentences below. Do the sentences include a definition
or a synonym? Write **D** for definition or **S** for synonym.

Wood mice build underground nests and **intricate**,
or complex, burrows.

The price of fruit is going up because of the **drought**
in California. A drought is a shortage of water.

Her **ancestors** travelled long distances. Ancestors are
the people in her family who lived before she was born.

The town will **ration**, or limit, its use of street salt,
so it will have enough for the forecasted snowstorm.

5 Underline the words in the sentences below that are given as examples
or comparisons to help you understand the words in **bold**.

At the aquarium, there are **sea mammals**,
such as dolphins and whales.

We will compare **novels**, such as
Matilda and *The Twits*.

The **baboon**, like the gorilla and chimpanzee,
is a social animal.

Many **products**, such as spacecraft and medical supplies, are
made in the United States.

Nocturnal animals, such as bats and owls, look for food in the dark.

More word meanings

Sometimes, you can work out
the meaning of a word from clues
in the text. Let's find out…

① Choose the correct synonyms for the words in **bold** from
the word box below.

discard	miserable	lingers	healthy

The weather forecast for next week is **dismal**. ....

Brown rice is more **nutritious** for you than white rice. ....

How could someone **abandon** such a cute dog? ....

My sister **dawdles** when she is feeling lazy. ....

② In some sentences, the meanings of words are suggested by contrasting
phrases. Underline the contrasting phrase in each sentence below.
Hint: look for "but", "however", "yet" and "even though".

I studied for hours, but I still failed the test.

Even though Sam is a novice, he came down the slope at full speed.

Allie fell twice, yet she went down the ramp on her skateboard.

Some animals cannot survive in harsh climates; however, others can adapt.

③ For each row, read the first word and unscramble the letters in the second
column to make a synonym of the word. Then write the synonym.

Word	Letters	Synonym
accurate	ccrrtoe	
novice	bgeinner	
adjust	padat	
determined	mmttcdieo	

Time filler:
Find out how well you know the words you've been working with on these two pages. Write a word that means the opposite of each word. For example, the opposite of "discard" is "save".

4 Look at the diagram below to understand the many ways of finding out the meaning of words in a sentence.

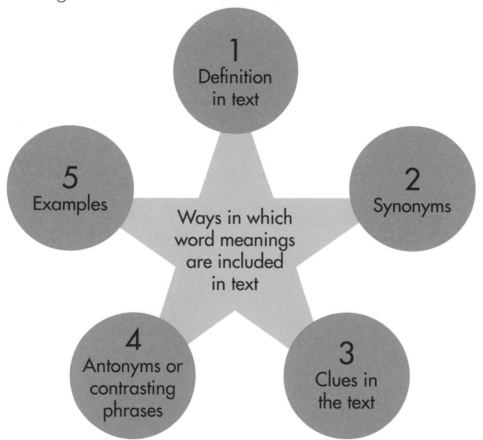

Now read the sentences. Then write the correct number from the diagram above that tells you how the meaning of each word in **bold** is shown.

People live in different kinds of **dwelling**, such as igloos and caves.

In a **triathlon**, people compete by running, swimming and cycling.

The city is planning to **demolish**, or tear down, the old train station.

That leftover pizza was **inedible**, so I had to discard it.

The recipe is **complicated**, but I can simplify it.

Shortened words

Some long words have shortened
forms. These shorter forms are
sometimes called clipped words.

① Draw a line from each word to its shortened form.

kilogram	exam
influenza	bike
gymnasium	flu
examination	kilo
bicycle	ad
advertisement	gym

② Write the long form for each of the shortened words below.

carbs ....

teen ....

fridge ....

phone ....

ref ....

stats ....

③ Pick either the word or its shortened form from the box to complete the sentences correctly.

> rhinoceros/rhino   spectacles/specs
>   veterinary/vet   photograph/photo

I took that .... with my phone.

I took Puggles to see the .... when he was ill.

A .... has a huge horn on its head.

I can't read the menu without my ....

Time filler:
See if you can find 10 examples
of shortened words in a magazine
or book. Ask family members
if they know any, too.

4) Read the complete form of each word and find its shortened form
in the word search. Then write the words next to their long forms.

a	p	l	a	n	e	p	g	h
m	a	t	h	s	d	e	l	i
o	g	y	m	e	r	d	a	g
p	h	i	p	p	o	w	b	r

mathematics ....

gymnasium ....

laboratory ....

hippopotamus ....

delicatessen ....

aeroplane ....

5) Blend words are formed by combining parts of two words.
Write the correct word from the box next to each pair of words.

smog	motel	brunch	moped

breakfast + lunch ....

motor + pedal ....

motor + hotel ....

smoke + fog ....

English language words

Learning terms used in reading and writing help you write and talk confidently about books and stories.

1 Draw a line from each word to its definition.

motive   note things that are different

moral   conclusion drawn based on facts

compare   reason for doing something

contrast   lesson to show what is the right behaviour

inference   note things that are similar

2 For each description below, write the element of a story from the box.

theme	character	setting	sequence	plot

talkative, friendly and outgoing   ....

courage, kindness and hope   ....

problem, events and solution   ....

what happens first, next and finally   ....

time and place of a story   ....

3 Draw a line from each kind of book to the reason you might need it.

encyclopedia   to look up the date of the next full moon

dictionary   to find information about the solar system

thesaurus   to find a map of Great Britain

almanac   to find the meaning of a word

atlas   to find a synonym for a word

Time filler:
Make a tiny flip book that lists terms you want to remember. Use examples to remind yourself of the meaning of the term, such as **alliteration: slithering snakes**.

4 Different types or styles of writing and books are called genres. To solve the crossword, read the clues to find different genres. **Hint:** the first letter of each answer has been provided.

Across
1. Book used for research and to find information
2. Book written about a real person
3. Story such as *Cinderella* or *Hansel and Gretel*
4. Type of book that has facts and informs (3-7)
5. Type of book in which characters look for clues to solve a problem

Down
1. Stories or novels
2. Literature that may or may not rhyme
3. A traditional story, often about ancient gods and monsters
4. Humorous books intended to make people laugh
5. Story that has a moral to teach a lesson

More English language words

Knowing the different types of sentence and how to vary them makes you a better writer. You will also read with a better understanding of the text.

(1) Sentences have different purposes.
A **declarative sentence** makes a statement.
An **interrogative sentence** asks a question.
An **imperative sentence** can be a command or a polite request.
An **exclamatory sentence** shows excitement or emotion.

Write "dec" for "declarative", "int" for "interrogative", "imp" for "imperative" or "ex" for "exclamatory" to describe each sentence.

Tony opened a new restaurant in town. ....

I haven't seen Tony in years! ....

Please tell me if you will be there. ....

Are you ordering pasta or pizza? ....

(2) Do you know a connective from an interjection or a preposition?
Connectives join words or groups of words.
Interjections express strong feelings.
Prepositions connect nouns to other words and often tell you where something or someone is.

Write the letter **C**, **I** or **P** to describe the underlined word in each sentence.

Jake went to the concert <u>and</u> he bought a poster.

<u>Please</u> stop pushing the lift button.

<u>On</u> each line, write the title and author of the book.

Mary <u>or</u> Jen will show you where the library is.

The shop <u>around</u> the corner sells fresh fruit and vegetables.

3 Different kinds of devices are used in writing. Read the numbered definitions to find out about these devices. Then number the sentences that follow to show which device is used in each sentence.

1. **Alliteration** is the use of words in the same phrase or sentence that begin with the same sound.
2. **Irony** is when something is not what was expected.
3. A **simile** compares one thing to another thing and uses the word "like" or "as".
4. A **metaphor** compares one thing to another without using the words "like" or "as".
5. **Dialogue** is the words spoken by people in a story or a play.

They waited 45 minutes to be served in a fast-food restaurant. ☐

That sharp metal edge is like a knife. ☐

The pretty princess picked up her pink parasol. ☐

Dave said, "Make sure you turn right at the light." ☐

4 Draw lines to match the words used to describe the stages of writing a book to their definitions.

Proofread   Background reading and note-taking about a topic

Draft   Release a book or a piece of writing to the public

Publish   An early version of a piece of writing or book

Research   Final check for errors of a book or piece of writing before it is published

Citizenship words

Citizenship studies has some specific words that are related to our government and our world. Learning those words will give you a better understanding of citizenship studies topics.

① Draw a line from each sentence to the title of the person who would say it.

I am the head of the government.   member of parliament

I am in charge of a village or town.   prime minister

I enforce the law and protect people.   mayor

I represent people in parliament.   police officer

② Choose the correct word from the box to complete each sentence below.

> vote   candidate   choosing   debate   election

Someone who is standing for office is a ....

People who are aged 18 and over can .... in an ....

When people vote in an election, they are .... a candidate.

Two candidates may discuss their political views in a ....

③ Read the clue and then unscramble the letters to write the correct word.

help from the government or other organisations
for people in need   ida   ....

beliefs, customs and traditions of a society   luuctre   ....

place or building in honour of a person or an event   mmnntoue   ....

a settlement bigger than a town   yitc   ....

Time filler:
Have a look in a newspaper or watch the news on TV. In a notebook, make a list of up to 10 words or phrases related to citizenship studies, such as "community" and "head of state", that you read or hear. Write their definitions alongside them. Use a dictionary to help you.

4 Draw a line from the definition to the word it defines.

things made by people who lived in the past   boundary

system of making and using goods   artifacts

limit or extent of a property or land   judge

person who leads the courtroom   assembly

people gathered for a common purpose   taxes

payments that support the government   economy

5 Read the clues to find the words needed to complete the crossword.
Hint: the first letter of each word has been provided.

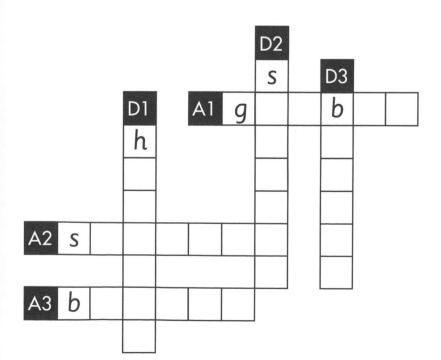

Across

1. Relating to the world
2. Person who makes a home in a new place
3. An imaginary line that defines the extent of an area such as a country

Down

1. An account of what happened in the past
2. Practice of owning people and forcing them to work
3. Exchange of goods and services for other goods and services

Useful word list 2

Read each column of words. Think about each word's meaning and then write a synonym on the line next to it. The first five have been done for you. Answers may vary.

annual	yearly	conscious	
answer	response	determine	
ascend	climb	disaster	
assist	aid	display	
astonish	astound	estimate	
attempt		exact	
attentive		existence	
attractive		extreme	
beneath		flexible	
blossom		frequently	
brilliant		glide	
burrow		graph	
centre		height	
complex		hindrance	

Time filler:
There may have been a few words on these two pages that you couldn't think of a synonym for or were unfamiliar to you. Look in a dictionary or a thesaurus to help you finish the activity.

imagine ....

inspire ....

interfere ....

invisible ....

journey ....

massive ....

miniature ....

mischief ....

numeral ....

occur ....

ought ....

overflow ....

probably ....

quarter ....

queue ....

recognise ....

research ....

separate ....

severe ....

stomach ....

superb ....

system ....

texture ....

thought ....

tradition ....

unite ....

vibrate ....

wriggle ....

Geography words

Words related to oceans, land masses
and our world can be classified as
geography words. Many of those
words are also related to science.

1 Choose the correct word from the box to complete each sentence below.

cliff	coast	oceans	continent	marsh

The land that borders the sea is the ....

A .... is a steep area of rock, often near the sea.

A massive area of land is a ....

A .... is an area of lowlands that is flooded.

Huge bodies of water that cover most of Earth's surface are ....

2 Cross out the word that is not related to the other words in each row.

river	cave	stream
country	city	hill
waterfall	desert	lake

3 Sort the words in the box into three groups of four below.
Then write a title for each group.

pond	eruption	magma	grasslands	rainforest	ocean
lava	crater	river	tundra	desert	lake

....

....
....
....
....

Time filler:
Many words related to geography are descriptions of different places and land forms around the world. Create a picture dictionary by listing 10 or more geography words and then drawing pictures of what the words represent to help you remember them.

(4) Choose the correct word from the box to match each description.

desert	island	climate	valley	glacier

low-lying area with slopes either side ....

weather conditions typical in a certain place ....

land that is surrounded by water ....

slow moving mass of ice ....

dry, barren area of land ....

(5) Read each definition in the first grid and then match it to the word in the second grid. Write the number of the word next to the correct letter.

A. water surrounded by land	D. relating to country life
B. relating to a city or town	E. period of no rain
C. imaginary line around Earth	F. pointed top of a mountain

1. urban	4. peak
2. rural	5. equator
3. lake	6. drought

A ....

C ....

E ....

B ....

D ....

F ....

Health words

Health and nutrition words help us know about our bodies and how they work. Learning about nutrition helps us know which types of food keep our bodies healthy.

① Read each description and choose the correct word from the box.

bacteria	broccoli	organic	digestion	calorie

This is an example of a food that contains vitamin C.

....

These can make people sick, but they are also used to make foods, such as yogurt.

....

This is a unit used to measure how much energy a particular food contains.

....

This is the process that breaks down food for the body to absorb and use.

....

This is a word used to describe foods grown without chemical pesticides or fertilisers.

....

② Draw a line from each definition to the word it describes.

nutrients, also called carbs, rich in energy and found in fruit and vegetables   calcium

nutrients found in plant and animal cells that we need to build body tissues   carbohydrates

mineral found in milk, yogurt, cheese and spinach that builds strong teeth and bones   grains

seeds of plants, such as corn, wheat and rice, used as food   proteins

Time filler:
Trace a picture of the human body from a book and label the external parts blue and the internal parts red. Then check a reference, such as an encyclopedia, to see how many parts you've got correct.

③ Read the descriptions and then find the words they describe in the word search. Finally, write the word on the dotted line for each description.

s	t	o	m	a	c	h	e	b	r	t	o	t	e	r
e	m	s	f	l	u	n	g	s	s	m	z	o	k	u
w	d	h	o	p	u	a	v	k	a	q	o	n	p	x
m	z	e	f	e	s	a	v	e	l	h	m	g	f	i
q	d	a	z	i	q	d	y	l	i	s	d	u	d	r
j	i	r	j	p	q	s	u	e	v	g	i	e	h	f
x	f	t	y	t	e	h	e	t	a	t	w	f	p	i
u	g	t	i	n	r	q	c	o	j	o	i	n	t	z
r	s	p	i	n	e	z	c	n	g	h	u	x	u	q

bones of the entire human body ....

fluid secreted in the mouth to help break down food ....

a place where two bones come together ....

this might rumble when a person is hungry ....

two organs in the chest used to breathe air ....

a muscular organ with taste buds in the mouth ....

an organ that expands and contracts to pump blood ....

a row of connected bones that protect the spinal cord ....

Maths words

Having problems understanding your problems? The words on these pages will help you top your maths class.

① Choose a word from the box to complete each row below.

> division   denominator   vertical   diameter   kilogram

horizontal   diagonal   ....

multiplication   subtraction   ....

weight   gram   ....

circumference   radius   ....

fraction   numerator   ....

② Read each word or phrase and understand its meaning.
Then unscramble the letters to fill in the blanks.

calculate   eovls   ....

half a circle   ircelcemis   ....

symmetrical winged insect   uettblrfy   ....

to find out the length of something   msrauee   ....

diagram showing information or data   arphg   ....

③ Draw a line from the word on the left to the correct information on the right.

dozen   1,000 metres

kilometre   distance from centre of a circle to its edge

litre   width x length of a flat surface

radius   1,000 millilitres

area   12 items

Time filler:
Create your own maths picture dictionary. Include words such as "rhombus", "diameter" and "angle". They will be easier to remember if you define them in your own words and draw pictures of them.

4 Write a word from the box to match each description below.

hectare	prime	calculate	array	metric

to work out an answer ....

a system that uses metres, kilograms and seconds ....

a unit used to measure land ....

rows and columns ....

number divided evenly only by one or itself ....

5 Draw a line from each description to the word it defines.

a fourth of something   pentagon

round shape   quarter

five-sided shape   circle

half of a sphere   adjacent

without an end   add

next to each other   infinite

to find a total   parallel

side by side with an equal   hemisphere
distance in between

Art and music words

Some terms are specifically used for art and music. Understanding those words will help you better appreciate the arts.

1 Read the words in the box below. Then sort them into the coloured boxes based on the titles. **Note:** one word below does not belong anywhere.

| impressionism | watercolour | abstract | paintings | sculptures |
| clay | oil paint | collages | melody | realism |

Styles of art

....
....
....

Materials to create art

....
....
....

Examples of art

....
....
....

2 Complete each sentence below with the correct word from the box.

| architecture | studio | exhibition | gallery |

A place where an artist might work is a ....

A place where art is displayed is a ....

A public showing of art is an ....

The art of designing buildings and other structures is ....

3 Write the correct art word from the box next to each description below.

| masterpiece | mural | abstract | portrait |

picture painted directly on a wall ....

picture of a person ....

an outstanding work of art ....

a work of art that is not realistic ....

Time filler:
Make a list of all the musical instruments you can think of. See if you can list at least 15 instruments. Ask a family member for help if you get stuck.

4) Draw a line from each music word to its description.

violinist	writes music
choir	leads an orchestra
composer	plays a violin
conductor	group of singers

5) Look at the diagram to learn about the parts of the guitar. Then answer the questions.

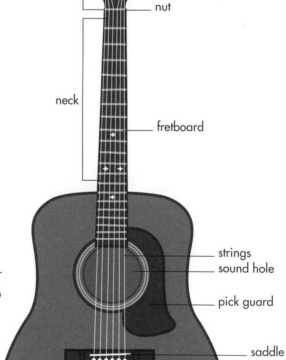

Which parts of the guitar produce sound?

....

Which parts of the guitar do you turn to adjust the strings?

....

Which part protects the body of the guitar from scratches when it is being strummed?

....

Which part of the guitar helps project its sound?

....

Sports words

You may be familiar with the
terms used in your favourite sport,
but it can be helpful to know some
of the words used in other sports, too.

(1) Write the name of the sport from the box next to each description.

| golf   basketball   football |

players aim to get a large ball
into a basket   ....

players must hit a small ball with
a club into 18 holes in the ground   ....

players aim to score goals by
kicking a round ball into a net   ....

(2) Choose the correct word to complete each sentence below.

Football is played on a ....   pitch/track

Basketball players score ....   hits/points

Teams should have a plan or a ....   strategy/trophy

(3) Choose the correct word from the box to complete each sentence below.

| goals   swimming   trophy   opponent   rowing |

Front crawl and breaststroke are examples of .... styles.

A tennis player serves the ball to the ....

Football players try to score ....

Winners at a tournament usually get a ....

Members of a .... team have to work together in their boat.

Time filler:
As you watch or read about a sport, list the words used that are specific to that sport in a notebook. For example, you may hear the word "deuce" during a tennis match and "offside" during a football match.

4 Read the sentences and then find the sport words they describe in the word search. Finally, write the words next to each of the descriptions.

t	p	p	t	e	n	n	i	s	h	e	a	d	g	x
f	e	o	p	n	y	q	m	b	a	a	o	r	t	s
e	o	v	o	q	o	m	n	l	b	n	v	m	k	t
i	i	m	o	n	q	e	s	f	e	n	c	i	n	g
e	w	c	l	a	v	y	k	f	z	y	u	t	e	x
i	q	p	n	l	q	i	i	l	h	e	b	t	n	m
t	k	s	b	a	s	k	e	t	b	a	l	l	o	n
g	x	g	l	j	f	x	r	a	r	c	h	e	r	y
s	a	s	d	u	f	r	f	x	o	b	h	m	s	e

Players use rackets to hit a ball over a net. ....

Players try to shoot an arrow into a target. ....

This is another word for a baseball glove. ....

A helmet is worn to protect this. ....

Water polo is played here. ....

Players fight using blunt-tipped blades. ....

This sport is played indoors on a court. ....

This person moves quickly down a slope. ....

Idioms and proverbs

Idioms are sayings that have meanings different from the words in the expression. Proverbs are short sayings that give some advice.

① Draw a line from each idiomatic sentence to its meaning.

That opened up a can of worms.	**Wait!**
Keep your chin up.	**You're annoying me.**
Pull your socks up!	**Stay positive.**
Hold your horses!	**That created a problem.**
You're getting on my nerves.	**You need to make an effort to improve.**

② Read the sentences in the table and then write the meaning of the idiom (underlined) by choosing words from the box.

annoying	nervous	unwell	get angry

Sentence	Meaning
She was <u>on tenterhooks</u>.	
The project was <u>a pain in the neck</u>.	
I am feeling <u>under the weather</u>.	
Don't <u>fly off the handle</u>.	

Time filler:
Write a few idiomatic expressions and draw pictures to illustrate the silliness of the meaning of the words. For example, if you are easily offended, you might be said to have "a chip on your shoulder".

3 Read the sentences first and then the proverbs in the table. Finally, write the number of the sentence that matches the proverb's meaning.

1. It seems to take longer when you keep waiting for something to happen.

2. Take your time and pace yourself so that you can finish.

3. Doing something over and over again helps you do it well.

4. It's better to deal with a problem now before it gets worse.

Proverb	Meaning
Practice makes perfect.	
A watched pot never boils.	
Slow and steady wins the race.	
A stitch in time saves nine.	

4 Pick the correct word from the box to complete the proverbs below.

stone	friend	castle	doctor

An apple a day keeps the .... away.

A friend in need is a .... indeed.

A man's home is his ....

A rolling .... gathers no moss.

Synonyms

Words that have the same or a similar meaning, such as "happy" and "content", are called synonyms.

1 Fill in the blanks in the table below with synonyms for each word. Use the word box to help you.

dire	soar	walked	awesome	enormous
nasty	huge	ascend	remarked	impressive
giant	scale	gigantic	journeyed	marvellous
large	awful	claimed	mentioned	despicable
go up	mount	travelled	proceeded	commented
horrid	called	departed	outstanding	extraordinary

bad	**great**	**big**
....	....	....
....	....	....
....	....	....
....	....	....
....	....	....
said	**went**	**climb**
....	....	....
....	....	....
....	....	....
....	....	....
....	....	....

Time filler:
See if you can think of five synonyms for each of the following words: "sad", "small", "wet", "cold", "hot", "quick", "food", "sleep", "eat" and "angry". Challenge your friends and family, too.

(2) For each word in the first column, write a synonym for it in the second column. Then write a sentence in the third column that includes the synonym.

Word	Synonym	Sentence
extinct		
limb		
festival		
transmit		
storm		
gather		
crooked		
rapidly		

Working with words

Improving your vocabulary
can make your writing much
more interesting.

(1) For each of the words in the first column, write which part of speech the
word is in the second column. Then write a sentence using the word in
the third column. **Hint:** some words can act as more than one part of
speech; for example, "venture" can be a noun or a verb.

Word	Part of speech	Sentence
alert		
awkward		
bleary		
flatter		
irritate		
observant		
scarcity		
venture		
weary		

Time filler:
Review some of the words that you're unfamiliar with in question 2. Look them up in a dictionary and then use them in sentences of your own to show that you understand their meaning.

② Think about the words you know well and the words you are not sure of. Try words from the box as a start. Fill in the blanks below. Look for other words on the useful word lists and do a similar exercise.

glide	aloud	exchange	surplus
disaster	complex	hideous	stale
partial	clumsy	depart	linger

Mmm…
I have seen it or heard it.

....
....
....
....

I have no clue.

....
....
....
....

I know it well.
I can use the word in a sentence.

....
....
....
....

Word practice

It is always helpful to practise the words you find difficult. It helps you learn their spelling, meaning and how to use them correctly.

① Some easily confused pairs of words are listed here. Write the words you don't know in the alphabet grid. List other words you have trouble with from the useful word lists in this book.

accept/except	practice/practise	moral/morale
their/there	precede/proceed	bought/brought
advice/advise	lose/loose	breathe/breath

A	B	C	D
E	F	G	H
I	J	K	L
M	N	O	P
Q	R	S	T
U	V	W	XYZ

Time filler:
Keep a diary of words that sound the same or look the same to you. For example, "through" and "though", "house" and "horse", "than" and "then", and others.

2) Aim to use adjectives! They help you describe words and experiences when you speak and write. Put an **X** in the box that each adjective might describe. Then write a sentence using the adjective. The first one has been done for you.

Adjective	Person	Place	Thing	Sentence
adventurous	✗		✗	The journey had been a long but adventurous one.
bitter				
confident				
gracious				
logical				
numerous				
slimy				
sparse				
successful				
urban				

Useful word list 3

Read each column of words. Think about each word's meaning and then write a synonym on the line next to it. The first five have been done for you. Answers may vary.

anxious	worried	essential	....
available	free	exchange	....
average	mean	fragile	....
bland	uninteresting	frontier	....
blizzard	snowstorm	glimpse	....
calamity	....	healthy	....
cemetery	....	hideous	....
content	....	intense	....
crater	....	interact	....
cruel	....	jut	....
deafening	....	labyrinth	....
definitely	....	linger	....
drama	....	logic	....
equip	....	loyal	....

Time filler:
There may have been a few words on these two pages that you couldn't think of a synonym for or were unfamiliar to you. Look in a dictionary or a thesaurus to help you finish the activity.

magnify	sculpture ....
mature	sphere ....
micro	suggest ....
migrate	symbol ....
miserable	theme ....
nuisance	thorough ....
party	thrive ....
peace	tingle ....
perimeter	total ....
population	transparent ....
portrait	universe ....
profession	urban ....
quarrel	verse ....
salute	vivid ....

Answers:

4–5 Words and their definitions
6–7 Antonyms

4

① Draw lines to match the words in the top row with the words that mean the same or almost the same in the bottom row.

exciting — thrilling
power — strength
choose — select
exchange — swap

② What does the underlined word in each sentence mean? Pick your answer from the box below.

| purchased | correct | grew well | a great number |

The farm produced an <u>abundance</u> of apples this year. — a great number
The apple trees <u>thrived</u> because of the rain. — grew well
We <u>bought</u> two baskets of apples. — purchased
Your description of the problem is <u>accurate</u>. — correct

③ Use words from the box to complete the sentences below.

| cupcake | lemon | sandpaper | snake | joke |

Something that tastes sour is a **lemon**.
Something that feels rough is **sandpaper**.
Something that is scrumptious is a **cupcake**.
Something that slithers is a **snake**.
Something that is amusing is a **joke**.

5

④ Read the first word in each row below. Then circle the two words in that row that mean the same as the first word.

end — (finish) part (conclude)
show — destroy (display) (demonstrate)

⑤ Read the clues below to complete the crossword puzzle. **Hint:** the first letter for each word in the crossword has been provided.

Crossword answers:
A1 linger, A2 rough, A3 capable, A4 destroy
D1 excellent, D2 repair, D3 glide, D4 rare

Across
1. To delay going somewhere
2. Having an irregular or uneven surface
3. Being able to do something
4. To wreck or ruin

Down
1. Very good
2. To mend something
3. To move smoothly and silently
4. Unusual

Whenever you are working with your child, encourage him or her to find the meaning of words from the text itself or from photos or illustrations that accompany the text. Doing this will help your child become a better, active reader who pays close attention to the text.

6

① Use words from the box to write an antonym for each word listed below.

| down | day | full | evening | dry | sad | fake | fiction |
| smooth | soft | bad | below | dark | serious | close | |

open — close   good — bad   up — down
real — fake   light — dark   hard — soft
funny — serious   night — day   rough — smooth
happy — sad   morning — evening   fact — fiction
above — below   empty — full   wet — dry

② Write the letter **A** in the box if the pairs of words are antonyms.

near/far [A]   lengthy/long [ ]
ask/answer [A]   hate/love [A]
little/small [ ]   narrow/thin [ ]
large/small [A]   baby/adult [A]

7

③ Write an antonym for the underlined word in each sentence. Answers may vary.

This watch was so <u>cheap</u>. — expensive
His drawing was colourful and <u>bright</u>. — dull
We drove down a <u>straight</u> country road. — winding
Did you have a good <u>morning</u>? — evening
Our group agreed to be <u>united</u>. — divided
The purple stone in my ring is a <u>common</u> one. — rare

④ Find an antonym for each of the clues below to solve the crossword puzzle. **Hint:** the first letter for each antonym has been given in the crossword.

Crossword answers:
A1 young, A2 highest, A3 give, A4 come
D1 polite, D2 tame

Across
1. old — young
2. lowest — highest
3. take — give
4. go — come

Down
1. rude — polite
2. wild — tame

Let your child pick a fictional or non-fictional passage to read with you. Highlight or list a few words from the passage. Ask your child to think of and write an antonym next to each of those words.

Answers:

8–9 Adjectives
10–11 Adverbs

8

① Read the story below. Then underline the 14 adjectives in it.

Baby's busy day

The prince and princess travelled to <u>faraway</u> places, where they met <u>large</u> crowds of <u>friendly</u> people. People always asked about their <u>adorable</u> baby. They would ask, "Where is <u>beautiful</u> Andrew?"

One day, the prince and princess took Andrew to visit babies. He wore a <u>blue</u> shirt and <u>white</u> trousers. He was <u>happy</u> to see all the <u>little</u> babies. He enjoyed playing with the <u>different</u> toys, too.

Then the prince and princess took Andrew home. He had had a <u>busy</u> day. He fell into a <u>deep</u> sleep. He dreamed about his <u>lovely</u> day and all his <u>new</u> friends.

Which adjectives in the story tell you about the size of something?
large, little

Which adjectives in the story describe Andrew?
adorable, beautiful, happy

② Choose the most suitable adjective from the box for each sentence.

| clumsy | noisy | sporty | lazy |

The ___noisy___ lawn mower woke me up.

My ___lazy___ dog likes to sleep all day.

Your new car is so ___sporty___, unlike your old piece of junk!

She was so ___clumsy___ that she bumped into the table.

9

③ Underline the adjective in each sentence below. Then write a word that means the same as that adjective. You can use a dictionary for help.
Answers may vary.

The <u>mischievous</u> puppy fell asleep on the sofa. ___naughty___

We could not work out the <u>cryptic</u> message he sent. ___mysterious___

The <u>miniature</u> doll's house had many rooms. ___small___

The <u>clever</u> children knew how to find help. ___bright___

④ Read the words in each box. Then underline the adjective.

<u>delicious</u>	illness	<u>elegant</u>	<u>brilliant</u>
damage	<u>illustrated</u>	effort	breathe
delete	isolate	electricity	branch
agitate	mystery	flake	squatter
<u>ancient</u>	<u>moist</u>	<u>filthy</u>	species
amuse	mingle	fever	<u>sensible</u>

Choose an adjective from above to match each definition below.

old	ancient	has pictures	illustrated
dazzling	brilliant	graceful	elegant
tasty	delicious	reasonable	sensible
slightly wet	moist	very dirty	filthy

Encourage your child to describe his or her day at school using specific adjectives. You could lead him or her on by asking questions, such as "How was your day?" and "What was difficult/happy/silly/unusual about your day?"

10

① Underline the adverb in each sentence. Then write "where", "how" or "when" to show the use of the adverb in that sentence.

My friend writes to me <u>often</u>. ___when___

Keila <u>boastfully</u> described her family holiday. ___how___

Did you travel <u>far</u> to get to the meeting? ___where___

Jack will come to the game <u>tomorrow</u>. ___when___

The little boy ate his ice cream <u>noisily</u>. ___how___

The dog barked so the birds flew <u>away</u>. ___where___

② Underline the adverb in each sentence. Then circle the word it modifies.

You can <u>easily</u> (make) a sandwich for lunch.

I like cereal but my sister <u>mostly</u> (eats) toast in the morning.

I <u>totally</u> (believe) what you say.

Let's (discuss) this <u>privately</u> in my room.

③ Draw lines to match each adjective to its adverb and then each adverb to its meaning.

Adjective	Adverb	Definition
day	daily	not clearly
obscure	privately	every day
private	obscurely	in a secret way

11

④ Read each sentence and underline the adverb in it. Then write each adverb under its description below.

Kevin <u>nervously</u> waited for his turn to spell the next word.

Jane had <u>never</u> been to an amusement park.

Franco <u>cheerfully</u> whistled as he walked home.

Gina played the piano <u>well</u> during her recital.

Paolo <u>quickly</u> ran across the road to get help from a policeman.

Dave <u>carelessly</u> ran on the wet floor and slipped.

rapidly	without care	not ever
quickly	carelessly	never
anxiously	happily	with skill
nervously	cheerfully	well

⑤ Change the words in the box to adverbs and use them to complete the sentences.

| loud | elegant | obvious | main |

The lady ___elegantly___ walked across the red carpet.

I didn't realise that I was speaking ___loudly___.

The land was ___mainly___ used for farming.

The team was ___obviously___ nervous about playing.

Guide your child to use adverbs to enhance his or her writing. When you review a story or homework written by him or her, correct all spelling and grammatical errors. Then demonstrate places where your child could add an adverb to go with a verb by asking **how**, **when** or **where** questions.

68

Answers:

12–13 Contractions
14–15 Comparisons

12 / **13**

1 Write the contraction for each pair of words.

she is	she's	you are	you're	does not	doesn't	I am	I'm
he is	he's	we are	we're	do not	don't	he would	he'd
it is	it's	they are	they're	there is	there's	let us	let's

2 Both "had" and "have" can be combined with different words to make contractions. Write the contraction for each combination.

had
- we had — we'd
- he had — he'd
- you had — you'd
- I had — I'd

have
- you have — you've
- they have — they've
- we have — we've
- I have — I've

3 Rewrite these sentences by changing each contraction into its long form.

I don't believe you.
I do not believe you.

You aren't concentrating on your work.
You are not concentrating on your work.

She hasn't called yet.
She has not called yet.

We aren't going to the party.
We are not going to the party.

4 Two friends are talking. How does their speech sound? Write the contraction for the underlined words in each sentence.

Maya: What is going on, Kate? — What's

Kate: My Dad is taking me to the new football pitch. — Dad's

Maya: That is a good idea. — That's

Kate: He is going to practise with me. It will be fun. Would you like to join us? — He's, It'll

Maya: I would love to! But I will have to ask my parents first. — I'd, I'll

Kate: Great! Let us talk later. — Let's

5 Contractions and possessives can be tricky to tell apart. "It's" is a contraction of "it is", whereas "its" shows possession, or ownership. Circle the correct word to complete each sentence below.

Whose / **Who's** going to the game?
Bob's / Bobs going to the game with me.
Its / **It's** the ticket for the game.
That's / Thats the team's logo.
There's / Theres no way to get there by train.

Write a silly note to your child and include several incorrectly spelled contractions in it. Ask him or her to first spot and then correct the errors. Review your child's understanding and knowledge of contraction usage and spelling. You could create word puzzles and games, as needed, to reinforce the concept of contractions.

14 / **15**

1 Analogies often appear this way: drop : rain :: flake : snow. They are read this way: drop is to rain as flake is to snow. Write the word from the box that correctly completes each analogy.

room   food   shoes   car

horse : carriage :: motor : car
hands : mittens :: feet : shoes
shovel : dirt :: fork : food
sky : Earth :: ceiling : room

2 Complete each analogy with the correct word from the box.

sad   sun   evening   down

Open is to close as up is to down.
Funny is to serious as happy is to sad.
Dark is to light as shade is to sun.
Dawn is to morning as dusk is to evening.

3 A metaphor is a comparison that does not use the word "like" or "as". Circle the words that tell what is being described in each metaphor.

The (road) was a blanket of snow.
My (teacher) is a walking encyclopedia.
Last night, the (motorway) was a car park.

4 A simile is a comparison that uses a word such as "like" or "as" to make the comparison. Find the words in the word search that complete the similes in the sentences below.

a	d	s	u	n	o	p	g	h	c	c	x	q
m	p	a	r	r	o	t	n	z	h	p	i	b
o	w	t	r	e	a	s	u	r	e	e	y	a
p	i	b	n	m	g	w	p	r	e	n	e	n
b	j	n	l	a	f	z	y	v	t	g	w	q
e	l	e	p	h	a	n	t	s	a	u	i	u
e	o	d	f	q	p	m	a	c	h	i	n	e
k	n	w	v	s	o	r	g	e	o	n	k	t

Her yellow dress is as bright as the sun.
She squawked like a parrot.
The museum collection is like hidden treasure.
They walked like a herd of elephants.
The team worked like a well-oiled machine.
He was as busy as a bee.
He ran as fast as a cheetah.
The little boy is walking like a penguin.
That lunch was like a banquet.

Grammatical devices such as analogies, similes and metaphors all help explain the meaning of words. They help us understand what the word represents in a particular context. Encourage your child to use these devices not only in his or her written work but also in his or her speech.

Answers:

16–17 Homographs
18–19 Concept words

16

1 Find and circle each pair of homographs in these pairs of sentences. Then underline the word that matches the definition on the right.

The (record) shows your licence has expired.
Did you (record) your brother's song?

[to reproduce sound]

The baby ran after the (ball).
He wore a tuxedo to the (ball).

[large, formal party]

2 Pick the correct homograph from the box to complete each pair of sentences below.

[tear   bow   date   present]

Tie a ___bow___ in your hair.
Be sure to ___bow___ after you perform.

More than 20 people were ___present___ at the meeting.
I want to open my birthday ___present___ now!

That is the ___date___ of my next dental appointment.
My brother is going on a ___date___ with Becky tonight.

Why did you ___tear___ the pages out of the magazine?
We could see the ___tear___ on the actor's cheek.

17

3 Draw a line to match the descriptions to the words they define. Each word on the right has two meanings.

a winged mammal and a piece of sporting equipment — bat
a drink to celebrate and browned slices of bread — toast
sweet dark fruit and a day and time — date
animal skin and to conceal — hide
not heavy and not dark — light

4 Use each word from the box twice to complete the story.

[fine   park   bark   left   right   lead]

Trip to the park

Today, Dad drove us to the ___park___. We ___left___ home after lunch. The weather was ___fine___. Ben, our dog, began to ___bark___ as Dad looked for somewhere to ___park___ the car. Dogs are allowed to run free in the park. In other public places, they must be kept on a ___lead___ or you might get a ___fine___. In the park, we let Ben ___lead___ the way to his favourite spot: the big pond. We came to a fork in the path by a big tree with reddish brown ___bark___. I wasn't sure whether to turn ___left___ or ___right___, but Ben knew which was the ___right___ way. Soon, we were at the pond and Ben had a good swim.

As an extension to the exercises on these pages, you could look in dictionary with your child to find homographs with several different meanings. Such words include "set" and "project". Can you find five homographs with three or more meanings?

18

1 In each column, circle one of the last two words to complete the group of concept words.

uncle	meadow	taxi	nose
father	field	train	mouth
brother	valley	bus	eyes
niece	(forest)	ferry	(ears)
(nephew)	river	(car)	toes

2 Cross out the word in each row that is not related to the others.

dog	horse	cow	~~shark~~
~~frog~~	butterfly	moth	bee
window	~~tree~~	roof	door

3 Fill in a word to complete each concept group. Answers may vary.

Subjects in school	Coverings for feet
history	shoes
maths	boots
science	sandals
English	slippers

4 Give a title to each of the two concept groups.

Insects	Birds
ant	hawk
bee	crow
butterfly	owl
moth	puffin

19

5 Sort these words into the four boxes below based on the concepts they refer to. Then write a title for each box.

[processor   mouse   chain   flower   wheels
farm   root   keyboard   spokes   monitor   handlebars
leaf   harvest   stem   crops   irrigation]

Farm words	Parts of a plant	Computer words	Parts of a bicycle
farm	root	keyboard	spokes
harvest	leaf	monitor	handlebars
crops	stem	processor	chain
irrigation	flower	mouse	wheels

6 Read the words in the boxes below. Write a title for each box.

Measurements of a circle	Parts of a horse
circumference	mane
diameter	forelock
radius	hoof
centre	tail

Concept boxes provide a visual way to study words related to the same theme. They can help your child study vocabulary for subjects such as science and geography. Draw sections inside a box or circle and write words related to a topic of study in each section. On small cards, write their synonyms or definitions. Help your child match the words to their synonyms or definitions.

Answers:

20–21 Shades of meaning
22–23 Useful word list 1, see p.80
24–25 Homophones

20

1 Choose the correct word from the box to complete each row.

| lukewarm | massive | angry | intelligent |

grumpy	cross	furious	_angry_
competent	smart	brilliant	_intelligent_
big	huge	immense	_massive_
tepid	warm	hot	_lukewarm_

2 Put the groups of words in the correct order from weakest to strongest. Write them from left to right in each row of boxes.

| cold, freezing, cool | furious, annoyed, angry | dirty, filthy, soiled |

annoyed → angry → furious
cool → cold → freezing
soiled → dirty → filthy

3 For each pair, circle the word that has a stronger meaning.

(astound) surprise | (soar) fly
trip (fall) | call (yell)
(boil) simmer | (slam) close

21

4 Solve the crossword puzzle below. The answers are close in their meaning to the clues. **Hint:** the first letter for each answer has been provided.

Across
1. icy
2. tired
3. be anxious
4. excited

Down
1. injured
2. sad
3. dislike
4. eat

A1 frozen
D3 l a t h
D2 m i (injured... hurt)
A2 exhausted
A3 worry
A4 thrilled

5 Pick words from the crossword above to complete the sentences below.

Our players were _thrilled_ when they beat the Royals.
Terry was _miserable_ when the match was cancelled.
She had to _devour_ her lunch before going to class.
I just _loathe_ having to clean my room.
Joan _hurt_ herself when she fell down the stairs.

Encourage your child to be clear and use accurate words when he or she is describing things or situations to you. Offer some options, if necessary, to show that different shades of meaning should be distinguished and that it is often possible to find a more suitable word to describe something.

24

1 Read the pairs of homophones in the box below. Then choose the correct homophone and write it next to its clue.

| whole/hole | aloud/allowed | scent/sent |
| piece/peace | week/weak | threw/through |

odour	_scent_	posted	_sent_	opening	_hole_
tossed	_threw_	entire	_whole_	feeble	_weak_
out loud	_aloud_	permitted	_allowed_	via	_through_
calm	_peace_	part of	_piece_	seven days	_week_

2 Read aloud the pairs of homophones in the box below. Then pick the correct homophone to complete each sentence. **Hint:** only six words are needed.

| grate/great | doe/dough | flour/flower | break/brake | days/daze |

Did you _grate_ the cheese?
The _days_ seemed to fly by during our holiday.
The lady placed a pink _flower_ in a blue vase on every table.
Joanna cried out when she saw her favourite toy _break_.
We used _flour_, eggs and milk to make the _dough_.

25

3 Read each homophone and the clue. Then complete the crossword puzzle. **Hint:** the first letter for each answer has been provided.

A1 night
A2 raise
A3 lone
A4 seam

Across
1. knight, evening
2. rays, increase
3. loan, one
4. seem, edge

Down
1. no, understand
2. horse, sounding husky
3. blew, colour
4. knows, we use it to smell
5. dew, owed

4 Complete the two charts below by writing the correct homophone for each word.

Word	Homophone
would	wood
threw	through
their	there

Word	Homophone
peak	peek
pale	pail
you're	your

With your child, read aloud *Aunt Ant Leaves through the Leaves* by Nancy Coffelt or *How Much Can a Bare Bear Bear?* by Brian P. Cleary. These homophone-packed stories will help you teach your child the importance of using the correct words.

Answers:

26–27 Visual information
28–29 Science words

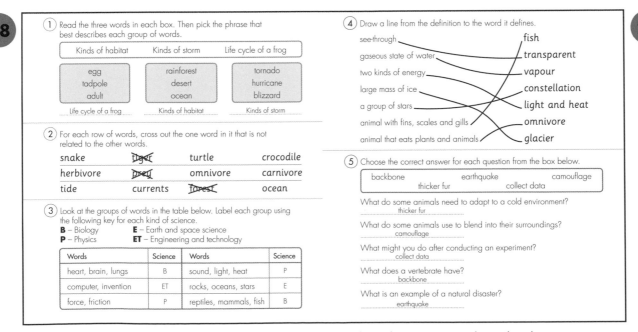

26

1 Look at the parts of a bicycle below. Then circle the correct answers in the questions that follow.

bell
handlebar
light
gear shifter
seat/saddle
frame
brake lever
cable
light
front brake
rear brake
fork
reflector
hub
rim
tyre
spokes
pedal
reflector
rear wheel
chain
front wheel

Which four parts of the bike are directly attached to the wheel?

(spoke) (rim) pedal (hub) (tyre) saddle

Where is the bell?
(on the handlebar)
on the chain

What is the centre of the wheel called?
(hub) rim

What is another name for the saddle?
tyre (seat)

What is the largest part of the bicycle?
wheel (frame)

27

2 Look at the parts of a sailing boat below. Then circle the correct answers to the questions that follow.

mast
mainsail
jib stay
backstay
boom
tiller
jib
stern
deck
rudder
bow
hull
keel

What is the front part of the boat called? stern (bow)

Which part of the boat holds up the sail? (mast) tiller

What is the larger sail on the boat called? jib (mainsail)

Which underwater part keeps the boat stable? jib (keel)

What is the main body of the boat known as? (hull) boom

Graphic or visual information is used all the time to convey information in a manner that is easy to understand. Make sure your child is able to read and understand annotated diagrams, such as the parts of the human body or parts of an electronic device.

28

1 Read the three words in each box. Then pick the phrase that best describes each group of words.

Kinds of habitat	Kinds of storm	Life cycle of a frog
egg tadpole adult	rainforest desert ocean	tornado hurricane blizzard
Life cycle of a frog	Kinds of habitat	Kinds of storm

2 For each row of words, cross out the one word in it that is not related to the other words.

snake ~~tiger~~ turtle crocodile
herbivore ~~prey~~ omnivore carnivore
tide currents ~~forest~~ ocean

3 Look at the groups of words in the table below. Label each group using the following key for each kind of science.
B – Biology   **E** – Earth and space science
P – Physics   **ET** – Engineering and technology

Words	Science	Words	Science
heart, brain, lungs	B	sound, light, heat	P
computer, invention	ET	rocks, oceans, stars	E
force, friction	P	reptiles, mammals, fish	B

29

4 Draw a line from the definition to the word it defines.

see-through ——— fish
gaseous state of water ——— transparent
two kinds of energy ——— vapour
large mass of ice ——— constellation
a group of stars ——— light and heat
animal with fins, scales and gills ——— omnivore
animal that eats plants and animals ——— glacier

5 Choose the correct answer for each question from the box below.

backbone	earthquake	camouflage
thicker fur		collect data

What do some animals need to adapt to a cold environment?
thicker fur

What do some animals use to blend into their surroundings?
camouflage

What might you do after conducting an experiment?
collect data

What does a vertebrate have?
backbone

What is an example of a natural disaster?
earthquake

One of the biggest challenges for young students is to read non-fiction books and, in particular, to understand science concepts. Help your child by playing games and puzzles or by creating word searches that incorporate words from the world of science.

Answers:

30–31 Word games
32–33 Word meanings

30

In each magic square game, read the clues in the first word grid. For each word, find its synonym or definition in the second word grid. Then write the number of that word next to the letter that matches it in the bottom grid. For example, the answer to the first clue, **A. precious**, is **2. valuable**, so **A2** is the first full answer in the bottom grid. Check your answers by making sure the numbers in the boxes add up to the same number horizontally, vertically and diagonally. Magical, isn't it?

(1) Magic square game 1

A. precious	B. confuse	C. uneven
D. model of the world	E. circular	F. bloom
G. attentive	H. delicate	I. go down

1. blossom	2. valuable	3. fragile
4. focused	5. round	6. jagged
7. perplex	8. descend	9. globe

A 2	B 7	C 6
D 9	E 5	F 1
G 4	H 3	I 8

(2) Magic square game 2

A. try	B. maintain	C. sturdy
D. conclude	E. delay	F. enclose
G. display	H. hysterical	I. foe

1. preserve	2. enemy	3. end
4. exhibit	5. postpone	6. strong
7. surround	8. attempt	9. frantic

A 8	B 1	C 6
D 3	E 5	F 7
G 4	H 9	I 2

Create a magic square game of your own to encourage your child to learn and use new words. Start with a box with nine sections. Assign each section a number so that the sum of the numbers is 15 vertically, horizontally and diagonally, as above. Then write the clues and answers.

32

(1) In each pair of sentences below, circle the word in **bold** and underline its meaning.

Our science teacher told us to wear long trousers to prevent bites from insects and (ticks) A tick is a tiny animal related to spiders.

Whales have (blubber) under their skin to keep them warm. Blubber is a thick layer of fat.

Some animals protect themselves through (mimicry). Using mimicry means copying the appearance, actions or sounds of another animal.

(2) In each sentence below, circle the word in **bold** and underline its meaning.

The storm caused a huge (surge) or wave of water, to flood the town.

The picture was (askew) or not straight, on the wall.

We hiked to the (summit) the highest point, of the trail.

(3) Underline the examples given to help you understand the subject of each sentence below.

Some rodents, including hamsters and gerbils, can be kept as pets.

Renewable energy, such as wind or solar power, comes from natural resources.

Some biomes, including rainforests and deserts, are home to unusual animals.

(4) Read the sentences below. Do the sentences include a definition or a synonym? Write **D** for definition or **S** for synonym.

Wood mice build underground nests and **intricate**, or complex, burrows. [S]

The price of fruit is going up because of the **drought** in California. A drought is a shortage of water. [D]

Her **ancestors** travelled long distances. Ancestors are the people in her family who lived before she was born. [D]

The town will **ration**, or limit, its use of street salt, so it will have enough for the forecasted snowstorm. [S]

(5) Underline the words in the sentences below that are given as examples or comparisons to help you understand the words in **bold**.

At the aquarium, there are **sea mammals**, such as dolphins and whales.

We will compare **novels**, such as Matilda and The Twits.

The **baboon**, like the gorilla and chimpanzee, is a social animal.

Many **products**, such as spacecraft and medical supplies, are made in the United States.

Nocturnal animals, such as bats and owls, look for food in the dark.

It is important that your child should always try to find the meaning of a word or clues about its meaning from the text before he or she looks it up in a dictionary.

Answers:

34–35 More word meanings
36–37 Shortened words

34

① Choose the correct synonyms for the words in **bold** from the word box below.

| discard | miserable | lingers | healthy |

The weather forecast for next week is **dismal**. — miserable

Brown rice is more **nutritious** for you than white rice. — healthy

How could someone **abandon** such a cute dog? — discard

My sister **dawdles** when she is feeling lazy. — lingers

② In some sentences, the meanings of words are suggested by contrasting phrases. Underline the contrasting phrase in each sentence below.
Hint: look for "but", "however", "yet" and "even though".

I studied for hours, but I still failed the test.

Even though Sam is a novice, he came down the slope at full speed.

Allie fell twice, yet she went down the ramp on her skateboard.

Some animals cannot survive in harsh climates; however, others can adapt.

③ For each row, read the first word and unscramble the letters in the second column to make a synonym of the word. Then write the synonym.

Word	Letters	Synonym
accurate	ccrrtoe	correct
novice	bgeinner	beginner
adjust	padat	adapt
determined	mmttcdieo	committed

35

④ Look at the diagram below to understand the many ways of finding out the meaning of words in a sentence.

Now read the sentences. Then write the correct number from the diagram above that tells you how the meaning of each word in **bold** is shown.

People live in different kinds of **dwelling**, such as igloos and caves. [5]

In a **triathlon**, people compete by running, swimming and cycling. [1]

The city is planning to **demolish**, or tear down, the old train station. [2]

That leftover pizza was **inedible**, so I had to discard it. [3]

The recipe is **complicated**, but I can simplify it. [4]

Guide your child to learn the meaning of words from the text at all times. Read *Dear Mr. Henshaw* by Beverly Cleary with your child. Provide him or her with a list of words to look out for while reading the book. These may include "amused", "argument", "dumb", "expecting", "rig" and "tractor".

36

① Draw a line from each word to its shortened form.

kilogram — kilo
influenza — flu
gymnasium — gym
examination — exam
bicycle — bike
advertisement — ad

② Write the long form for each of the shortened words below.

carbs — carbohydrates
teen — teenage/teenager
fridge — refrigerator
phone — telephone
ref — referee
stats — statistics

③ Pick either the word or its shortened form from the box to complete the sentences correctly. Answers may vary.

| rhinoceros/rhino | spectacles/specs |
| veterinary/vet | photograph/photo |

I took that photograph/photo with my phone.

I took Puggles to see the veterinary/vet when he was ill.

A rhinoceros/rhino has a huge horn on its head.

I can't read the menu without my spectacles/specs.

37

④ Read the complete form of each word and find its shortened form in the word search. Then write the words next to their long forms.

a	p	l	a	n	e	p	g	h
m	a	t	h	s	d	e	l	i
o	g	y	m	e	r	d	a	g
p	h	i	p	p	o	w	b	r

mathematics — maths
gymnasium — gym
laboratory — lab
hippopotamus — hippo
delicatessen — deli
aeroplane — plane

⑤ Blend words are formed by combining parts of two words. Write the correct word from the box next to each pair of words.

| smog | motel | brunch | moped |

breakfast + lunch — brunch
motor + pedal — moped
motor + hotel — motel
smoke + fog — smog

Introduce your child to the origin or history of shortened words that are commonly used today. This can sometimes make it easier for him or her to understand the meaning of certain words. For example: "typo/typographical error", "tie/necktie", "phone/telephone" and "flu/influenza".

Answers:

38–39 English language words
40–41 More English language words

---

38 **39**

① Draw a line from each word to its definition.

motive — reason for doing something
moral — lesson to show what is the right behaviour
compare — note things that are similar
contrast — note things that are different
inference — conclusion drawn based on facts

② For each description below, write the element of a story from the box.

| theme | character | setting | sequence | plot |

talkative, friendly and outgoing .... character
courage, kindness and hope .... theme
problem, events and solution .... plot
what happens first, next and finally .... sequence
time and place of a story .... setting

③ Draw a line from each kind of book to the reason you might need it.

encyclopedia — to find information about the solar system
dictionary — to find the meaning of a word
thesaurus — to find a synonym for a word
almanac — to look up the date of the next full moon
atlas — to find a map of Great Britain

④ Different types or styles of writing and books are called genres. To solve the crossword, read the clues to find different genres. **Hint:** the first letter of each answer has been provided.

Crossword answers:
A1 reference
A2 biography
A3 fairytale
A4 nonfiction
D2 (across A5) mystery
D1 fiction
D3 comedy
D4 comedy
D5 fable

Across
1. Book used for research and to find information
2. Book written about a real person
3. Story such as *Cinderella* or *Hansel and Gretel*
4. Type of book that has facts and informs (3-7)
5. Type of book in which characters look for clues to solve a problem

Down
1. Stories or novels
2. Literature that may or may not rhyme
3. A traditional story, often about ancient gods and monsters
4. Humorous books intended to make people laugh
5. Story that has a moral to teach a lesson

Share with your child different types of reading material, such as cookbooks, magazines and story books. Ask your child to point out some examples of the different types of sentence as outlined in question 1 on page 40.

---

40 **41**

① Sentences have different purposes.
A **declarative sentence** makes a statement.
An **interrogative sentence** asks a question.
An **imperative sentence** can be a command or a polite request.
An **exclamatory sentence** shows excitement or emotion.

Write "dec" for "declarative", "int" for "interrogative", "imp" for "imperative" or "ex" for "exclamatory" to describe each sentence.

Tony opened a new restaurant in town. .... dec
I haven't seen Tony in years! .... ex
Please tell me if you will be there. .... imp
Are you ordering pasta or pizza? .... int

② Do you know a connective from an interjection or a preposition?
Connectives join words or groups of words.
Interjections express strong feelings.
Prepositions connect nouns to other words and often tell you where something or someone is.

Write the letter **C**, **I** or **P** to describe the underlined word in each sentence.

Jake went to the concert <u>and</u> he bought a poster. — C
<u>Please</u> stop pushing the lift button. — I
<u>On</u> each line, write the title and author of the book. — P
Mary <u>or</u> Jen will show you where the library is. — C
The shop <u>around</u> the corner sells fresh fruit and vegetables. — P

③ Different kinds of devices are used in writing. Read the numbered definitions to find out about these devices. Then number the sentences that follow to show which device is used in each sentence.
1. **Alliteration** is the use of words in the same phrase or sentence that begin with the same sound.
2. **Irony** is when something is not what was expected.
3. A **simile** compares one thing to another thing and uses the word "like" or "as".
4. A **metaphor** compares one thing to another without using the words "like" or "as".
5. **Dialogue** is the words spoken by people in a story or a play.

They waited 45 minutes to be served in a fast-food restaurant. — 2
That sharp metal edge is like a knife. — 3
The pretty princess picked up her pink parasol. — 1
Dave said, "Make sure you turn right at the light." — 5

④ Draw lines to match the words used to describe the stages of writing a book to their definitions.

Proofread — Final check for errors of a book or piece of writing before it is published
Draft — An early version of a piece of writing or book
Publish — Release a book or a piece of writing to the public
Research — Background reading and note-taking about a topic

These pages include only some of the terms people use when discussing English language. Knowing these terms will help your child understand the different purposes of sentences, the types of words used in sentences and figures of speech.

Answers:

42–43 Citizenship words
44–45 Useful word list 2, see p.80
46–47 Geography words

42

1 Draw a line from each sentence to the title of the person who would say it.

I am the head of the government. — member of parliament
I am in charge of a village or town. — prime minister
I enforce the law and protect people. — mayor
I represent people in parliament. — police officer

2 Choose the correct word from the box to complete each sentence below.

| vote | candidate | choosing | debate | election |

Someone who is standing for office is a __candidate__ .

People who are aged 18 and over can __vote__ in an __election__ .

When people vote in an election, they are __choosing__ a candidate.

Two candidates may discuss their political views in a __debate__ .

3 Read the clue and then unscramble the letters to write the correct word.

help from the government or other organisations
for people in need   ida   __aid__

beliefs, customs and traditions of a society   luuctre   __culture__

place or building in honour of a person or an event   mmnntoue   __monument__

a settlement bigger than a town   yitc   __city__

43

4 Draw a line from the definition to the word it defines.

things made by people who lived in the past — boundary
system of making and using goods — artifacts
limit or extent of a property or land — judge
person who leads the courtroom — assembly
people gathered for a common purpose — taxes
payments that support the government — economy

5 Read the clues to find the words needed to complete the crossword.
Hint: the first letter of each word has been provided.

Crossword:
A1 g l o b a l
A2 s e t t l e r
A3 b o r d e r
D1 h i s t o r y
D2 s l a v e r y
D3 b a r t e r

Across
1. Relating to the world
2. Person who makes a home in a new place
3. An imaginary line that defines the extent of an area such as a country

Down
1. An account of what happened in the past
2. Practice of owning people and forcing them to work
3. Exchange of goods and services for other goods and services

Discuss with your child how your country is governed. Do you have a president, a prime minister or both? Do you have a congress or a parliament? What do you call the people elected to represent the citizens of your country?

46

1 Choose the correct word from the box to complete each sentence below.

| cliff | coast | oceans | continent | marsh |

The land that borders the sea is the __coast__ .

A __cliff__ is a steep area of rock, often near the sea.

A massive area of land is a __continent__ .

A __marsh__ is an area of lowlands that is flooded.

Huge bodies of water that cover most of Earth's surface are __oceans__ .

2 Cross out the word that is not related to the other words in each row.

river	~~lake~~	stream
country	city	~~hill~~
waterfall	~~desert~~	lake

3 Sort the words in the box into three groups of four below.
Then write a title for each group. Answers may vary.

| pond | eruption | magma | grasslands | rainforest | ocean |
| lava | crater | river | tundra | desert | lake |

Volcano words	Bodies of water	Habitats
crater	pond	grasslands
magma	ocean	rainforest
lava	river	desert
eruption	lake	tundra

47

4 Choose the correct word from the box to match each description.

| desert | island | climate | valley | glacier |

low-lying area with slopes either side   __valley__

weather conditions typical in a certain place __climate__

land that is surrounded by water   __island__

slow moving mass of ice   __glacier__

dry, barren area of land   __desert__

5 Read each definition in the first grid and then match it to the word in the second grid. Write the number of the word next to the correct letter.

A. water surrounded by land	D. relating to country life
B. relating to a city or town	E. period of no rain
C. imaginary line around Earth	F. pointed top of a mountain

1. urban	4. peak
2. rural	5. equator
3. lake	6. drought

A __3__   C __5__   E __6__
B __1__   D __2__   F __4__

Studies show that children need to read or hear a new word several times before they can recall its meaning. Reviewing the words on pages 46–47, ask your child to use three different highlighters to indicate the words that represent land, the words that represent water and other words that are unrelated.

Answers:

48–49 Health words
50–51 Maths words

48

1 Read each description and choose the correct word from the box.

| bacteria | broccoli | organic | digestion | calorie |

This is an example of a food that contains vitamin C. ....broccoli....

These can make people sick, but they are also used to make foods, such as yogurt. ....bacteria....

This is a unit used to measure how much energy a particular food contains. ....calorie....

This is the process that breaks down food for the body to absorb and use. ....digestion....

This is a word used to describe foods grown without chemical pesticides or fertilisers. ....organic....

2 Draw a line from each definition to the word it describes.

nutrients, also called carbs, rich in energy and found in fruit and vegetables — *calcium*

nutrients found in plant and animal cells that we need to build body tissues — *carbohydrates*

mineral found in milk, yogurt, cheese and spinach that builds strong teeth and bones — *grains*

seeds of plants, such as corn, wheat and rice, used as food — *proteins*

49

3 Read the descriptions and then find the words they describe in the word search. Finally, write the word on the dotted line for each description.

s	t	o	m	a	c	h	e	b	r	t	o	t	e	r
e	m	s	f	l	u	n	g	s	s	m	z	o	k	u
w	d	h	o	p	u	a	v	k	a	q	o	n	p	x
m	z	e	f	e	s	a	v	e	l	h	m	g	f	i
q	d	a	z	i	q	d	y	l	i	s	d	u	d	r
j	i	r	j	p	q	s	u	e	v	g	i	e	h	f
x	f	t	y	t	e	h	e	t	a	t	w	f	p	i
u	g	t	i	n	r	q	c	o	j	o	i	n	t	z
r	s	p	i	n	e	z	c	n	g	h	u	x	u	q

bones of the entire human body ....skeleton....
fluid secreted in the mouth to help break down food ....saliva....
a place where two bones come together ....joint....
this might rumble when a person is hungry ....stomach....
two organs in the chest used to breathe air ....lungs....
a muscular organ with taste buds in the mouth ....tongue....
an organ that expands and contracts to pump blood ....heart....
a row of connected bones that protect the spinal cord ....spine....

Encourage your child to read labels on foods. Point out healthy ingredients and those additives that should be limited. Emphasise the importance of eating foods that are less processed, such as fresh fruit and vegetables. Tell your child that those foods are healthier for you than many packaged and fast foods.

50

1 Choose a word from the box to complete each row below.

| division | denominator | vertical | diameter | kilogram |

horizontal	diagonal	....vertical....
multiplication	subtraction	....division....
weight	gram	....kilogram....
circumference	radius	....diameter....
fraction	numerator	....denominator....

2 Read each word or phrase and understand its meaning. Then unscramble the letters to fill in the blanks.

calculate	eovls	....solve....
half a circle	ircelcemis	....semicircle....
symmetrical winged insect	uettblrfy	....butterfly....
to find out the length of something	msrauee	....measure....
diagram showing information or data	arphg	....graph....

3 Draw a line from the word on the left to the correct information on the right.

dozen — 12 items
kilometre — 1,000 metres
litre — 1,000 millilitres
radius — distance from centre of a circle to its edge
area — width x length of a flat surface

51

4 Write a word from the box to match each description below.

| hectare | prime | calculate | array | metric |

to work out an answer ....calculate....
a system that uses metres, kilograms and seconds ....metric....
a unit used to measure land ....hectare....
rows and columns ....array....
number divided evenly only by one or itself ....prime....

5 Draw a line from each description to the word it defines.

a fourth of something — *quarter*
round shape — *circle*
five-sided shape — *pentagon*
half of a sphere — *hemisphere*
without an end — *infinite*
next to each other — *adjacent*
to find a total — *add*
side by side with an equal distance in between — *parallel*

Play a game in which your child estimates the length and width of objects to help build his or her appreciation of maths. Encourage him or her to read books that use maths as a theme. *Betcha* is a story of two friends who walk through town guessing the quantity of things around them. *Lemonade for Sale* is a story of children selling lemonade and using a graph to keep track of their sales. Both books are written by Stuart J. Murphy.

Answers:

52–53 Art and music words
54–55 Sports words

52

1 Read the words in the box below. Then sort them into the coloured boxes based on the titles. **Note:** one word below does not belong anywhere.

> impressionism   watercolour   abstract   paintings   sculptures
> clay   oil paint   collages   melody   realism

Styles of art	Materials to create art	Examples of art
abstract	clay	paintings
realism	oil paint	collages
impressionism	watercolour	sculptures

2 Complete each sentence below with the correct word from the box.

> architecture   studio   exhibition   gallery

A place where an artist might work is a   studio   .

A place where art is displayed is a   gallery   .

A public showing of art is an   exhibition   .

The art of designing buildings and other structures is   architecture   .

3 Write the correct art word from the box next to each description below.

> masterpiece   mural   abstract   portrait

picture painted directly on a wall   mural

picture of a person   portrait

an outstanding work of art   masterpiece

a work of art that is not realistic   abstract

53

4 Draw a line from each music word to its description.

violinist — plays a violin
choir — group of singers
composer — writes music
conductor — leads an orchestra

5 Look at the diagram to learn about the parts of the guitar. Then answer the questions.

head — tuning pegs, nut
neck — fretboard
strings, sound hole, pick guard, saddle, bridge, body

Which parts of the guitar produce sound?
   strings

Which parts of the guitar do you turn to adjust the strings?
   tuning pegs

Which part protects the body of the guitar from scratches when it is being strummed?
   pick guard

Which part of the guitar helps project its sound?
   sound hole

Discuss different forms of art and the term "appreciation of art" with your child. Explain that art represents a person's imagination, creative ideas and skills in a visual form, such as a painting or sculpture. You can do the same for music by asking your child to discuss his or her favourite songs and the genres they belong to.

54

1 Write the name of the sport from the box next to each description.

> golf   basketball   football

players aim to get a large ball into a basket   basketball

players must hit a small ball with a club into 18 holes in the ground   golf

players aim to score goals by kicking a round ball into a net   football

2 Choose the correct word to complete each sentence below.

Football is played on a   pitch   .   pitch/track

Basketball players score   points   .   hits/points

Teams should have a plan or a   strategy   .   strategy/trophy

3 Choose the correct word from the box to complete each sentence below.

> goals   swimming   trophy   opponent   rowing

Front crawl and breaststroke are examples of   swimming   styles.

A tennis player serves the ball to the   opponent   .

Football players try to score   goals   .

Winners at a tournament usually get a   trophy   .

Members of a   rowing   team have to work together in their boat.

55

4 Read the sentences and then find the sport words they describe in the word search. Finally, write the words next to each of the descriptions.

t	p	p	t	e	n	n	i	s	h	e	a	d	g	x
f	e	o	p	n	y	q	m	b	a	a	o	r	t	s
e	o	v	o	q	o	m	n	l	b	n	v	m	k	t
i	i	m	o	n	q	e	s	f	e	n	c	i	n	g
e	w	c	l	a	v	y	k	f	z	y	u	t	e	x
i	q	p	n	l	q	i	l	h	e	b	t	n	m
t	k	s	b	a	s	k	e	t	b	a	l	l	o	n
g	x	g	l	j	f	x	r	a	r	c	h	e	r	y
s	a	s	d	u	f	r	f	x	o	b	h	m	s	e

Players use rackets to hit a ball over a net.   tennis

Players try to shoot an arrow into a target.   archery

This is another word for a baseball glove.   mitt

A helmet is worn to protect this.   head

Water polo is played here.   pool

Players fight using blunt-tipped blades.   fencing

This sport is played indoors on a court.   basketball

This person moves quickly down a slope.   skier

Try this game with your child: describe a fact about a sport by using a phrase. For example, "I am thinking of a sport that has the largest ball used in any kind of sport." (basketball) or "I am thinking of a sport in which players cannot touch the ball with their hands." (football). Increase the level of difficulty based on your child's prior knowledge of sports.

Answers:

56–57 Idioms and proverbs
58–59 Synonyms

56

① Draw a line from each idiomatic sentence to its meaning.

That opened up a can of worms.	Wait!
Keep your chin up.	You're annoying me.
Pull your socks up!	Stay positive.
Hold your horses!	That created a problem.
You're getting on my nerves.	You need to make an effort to improve.

② Read the sentences in the table and then write the meaning of the idiom (underlined) by choosing words from the box.

annoying	nervous	unwell	get angry

Sentence	Meaning
She was <u>on tenterhooks</u>.	nervous
The project was <u>a pain in the neck</u>.	annoying
I am feeling <u>under the weather</u>.	unwell
Don't <u>fly off the handle</u>.	get angry

Idiomatic expressions can sound silly to children who are not used to hearing them. Many expressions are now outdated and rarely used in conversations. Help

57

③ Read the sentences first and then the proverbs in the table. Finally, write the number of the sentence that matches the proverb's meaning.

1. It seems to take longer when you keep waiting for something to happen.
2. Take your time and pace yourself so that you can finish.
3. Doing something over and over again helps you do it well.
4. It's better to deal with a problem now before it gets worse.

Proverb	Meaning
Practice makes perfect.	3
A watched pot never boils.	1
Slow and steady wins the race.	2
A stitch in time saves nine.	4

④ Pick the correct word from the box to complete the proverbs below.

stone	friend	castle	doctor

An apple a day keeps the _____doctor_____ away.

A friend in need is a _____friend_____ indeed.

A man's home is his _____castle_____ .

A rolling _____stone_____ gathers no moss.

your child understand idioms and proverbs by using such expressions and explaining their meaning.

58

① Fill in the blanks in the table below with synonyms for each word. Use the word box to help you.

dire	soar	walked	awesome	enormous
nasty	huge	ascend	remarked	impressive
giant	scale	gigantic	journeyed	marvellous
large	awful	claimed	mentioned	despicable
go up	mount	travelled	proceeded	commented
horrid	called	departed	outstanding	extraordinary

bad	**great**	**big**
awful	impressive	giant
horrid	awesome	huge
nasty	extraordinary	enormous
dire	marvellous	large
despicable	outstanding	gigantic

said	**went**	**climb**
mentioned	travelled	scale
claimed	proceeded	ascend
remarked	departed	soar
called	journeyed	mount
commented	walked	go up

As you review your child's homework, check his or her writing to make sure the same word, or words,

59

② For each word in the first column, write a synonym for it in the second column. Then write a sentence in the third column that includes the synonym. Answers may vary.

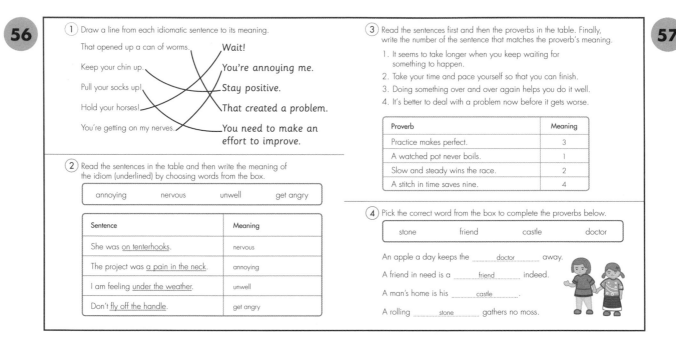

Word	Synonym	Sentence
extinct		
limb		
festival		
transmit		
storm		
gather		
crooked		
rapidly		

is not used repetitively. Suggest a variety of synonyms, whenever necessary, to improve his or her writing.

Answers:

60–61 Working with words
62–63 Word practice
64–65 Useful word list 3, see p.80

60

① For each of the words in the first column, write which part of speech the word is in the second column. Then write a sentence using the word in the third column. **Hint:** some words can act as more than one part of speech; for example, "venture" can be a noun or a verb.
Answers may vary.

Word	Part of speech	Sentence
alert		
awkward		
bleary		
flatter		
irritate		
observant		
scarcity		
venture		
weary		

61

② Think about the words you know well and the words you are not sure of. Try words from the box as a start. Fill in the blanks below. Look for other words on the useful word lists and do a similar exercise.
Answers may vary.

glide	aloud	exchange	surplus
	disaster	complex	hideous	stale
partial	clumsy	depart	linger

Mmm… I have seen it or heard it.	I have no clue.
....	....
....	....
....	....
....	....

I know it well.
I can use the word in a sentence.
....
....
....
....

Make copies of this page or use index cards to give your child some practice in working with new words. Encourage creativity by letting him or her write silly sentences, jokes or puns. Be around to help him or her understand the meaning of any new words and their correct usage.

62

① Some easily confused pairs of words are listed here. Write the words you don't know in the alphabet grid. List other words you have trouble with from the useful word lists in this book. Answers may vary.

accept/except	practice/practise	moral/morale
their/there	precede/proceed	bought/brought
advice/advise	lose/loose	breathe/breath

A	B	C	D
E	F	G	H
I	J	K	L
M	N	O	P
Q	R	S	T
U	V	W	XYZ

63

② Aim to use adjectives! They help you describe words and experiences when you speak and write. Put an **X** in the box that each adjective might describe. Then write a sentence using the adjective. The first one has been done for you. Answers may vary.

Adjective	Person	Place	Thing	Sentence
adventurous	**X**		**X**	The journey had been a long but adventurous one.
bitter				
confident				
gracious				
logical				
numerous				
slimy				
sparse				
successful				
urban				

As you review your child's homework, point out any errors in spelling and word usage. Explain to your child that all writers need an editor to review their writing.

Create word searches using adjectives and games using synonyms or definitions as clues.

80

Answers:

22–23 Useful word list 1
44–45 Useful word list 2
64–65 Useful word list 3

22

accurate	correct	dainty	delicate	increase	grow	possess	own
actual	real	damage	harm	jagged	spiky	recent	new
adjust	alter	decrease	lessen	lagoon	lake	region	area
advice	help	depth	deepness	marvel	wonder	regular	even
affect	influence	difficult	hard	narrator	storyteller	remember	recall
baffle	confuse	educate	teach	nation	country	scent	fragrance
baggage	luggage	effort	attempt	observe	watch	seize	grab
catalogue	list	emotion	feeling	occasion	event	strange	unusual
caution	care	fatal	deadly	odour	smell	strength	power
certain	sure	generous	kind	official	formal	tablet	slab
chief	head	glisten	shine	often	frequently	value	worth
circular	round	guide	steer	pardon	excuse	vapour	mist
clumsy	awkward	harsh	jarring	permit	allow	weary	tired
daily	everyday	illustrate	draw	phrase	expression	wreck	ruin

23

These pages list a variety of useful words that can help your child in his or her work. Make sure he or she gets into the habit of learning new words and then writing them down. Encourage your child to look at these lists frequently until he or she is confident in using the words. Each time, praise any progress or improvement he or she has made. Examples of synonyms have been supplied. Answers will undoubtedly vary because many of these words have more than one synonym or meaning and also because many of these words are used as more than one part of speech.

44

annual	yearly	conscious	aware	imagine	picture	queue	line
answer	response	determine	calculate	inspire	stimulate	recognise	know
ascend	climb	disaster	catastrophe	interfere	meddle	research	investigate
assist	aid	display	show	invisible	unseen	separate	divide
astonish	astound	estimate	guess	journey	trip	severe	harsh
attempt	try	exact	precise	massive	immense	stomach	belly
attentive	alert	existence	life	miniature	tiny	superb	excellent
attractive	pretty	extreme	severe	mischief	naughtiness	system	method
beneath	under	flexible	bendy	numeral	number	texture	feel
blossom	bloom	frequently	often	occur	happen	thought	idea
brilliant	dazzling	glide	slide	ought	should	tradition	custom
burrow	tunnel	graph	chart	overflow	spill	unite	join
centre	middle	height	tallness	probably	perhaps	vibrate	shake
complex	complicated	hindrance	obstacle	quarter	fourth	wriggle	squirm

45

64

anxious	worried	essential	vital	magnify	enlarge	sculpture	carving
available	free	exchange	swap	mature	adult	sphere	ball
average	mean	fragile	delicate	micro	tiny	suggest	recommend
bland	uninteresting	frontier	boundary	migrate	move	symbol	sign
blizzard	snowstorm	glimpse	notice	miserable	unhappy	theme	subject
calamity	disaster	healthy	well	nuisance	pest	thorough	rigorous
cemetery	graveyard	hideous	horrific	party	celebration	thrive	prosper
content	happy	intense	passionate	peace	quiet	tingle	prickle
crater	hollow	interact	communicate	perimeter	circumference	total	complete
cruel	brutal	jut	protrude	population	people	transparent	see-through
deafening	thunderous	labyrinth	maze	portrait	painting	universe	cosmos
definitely	absolutely	linger	remain	profession	career	urban	city
drama	play	logic	reason	quarrel	argue	verse	poetry
equip	provide	loyal	faithful	salute	greet	vivid	bright

65